RECEIVING AND MAINTAINING GOD'S REVIVAL IN YOUR LIFE AND IN THE LOCAL CHURCH

VOLUME 2

KNOWING SOME OF THE IMPORTANT REASONS AND THE DIVINE POWER BEHIND ALL REVIVALS

STEPHEN ADU-BOAHEN

TABLE OF CONTENTS

INTRODUCTION iv

CHAPTER ONE 1

SOME HUMAN REASONS WHICH MAKE CONTINUOUS PERSONAL AND GROUP REVIVALS STILL NECESSARY IN THE CHURCH OF CHRIST TODAY 1

CHAPTER TWO 41

SOME PRACTICAL AND THEOLOGICAL REASONS WHICH MAKE CONTINUOUS PERSONAL AND GROUP REVIVALS STILL NECESSARY IN THE CHURCH OF CHRIST TODAY 41

CHAPTER THREE 96

THE DIVINE SOURCE OF ALL TRUE REVIVALS IN THE CHURCH OF CHRIST. 96

CHAPTER FOUR 133

THE WORD OF GOD AND GOD'S REVIVALS 133

INTRODUCTION

Undertaking a journey without first knowing exactly where you are going can be some of the most unfortunate and unthinkable mistakes in life. Similarly, studying and going through lessons on God's revivals without knowing some of the most important reasons behind them as well as the divine sources of power behind these great spiritual awakenings can be most unfortunate and in some ways totally misleading. The purpose of this book, "knowing some of the important reasons and the divine power behind all revivals" is to help us to avoid this ridiculous mistake. Logically, to approach the subject of God's revivals with seriousness, we must first know their importance in God's economy and their great value in the life of the church.

Furthermore, we must know the specific sections of the word of God which expound and talk about them as well as the divine power behind them which makes it possible for them to be actualized and to be able to recur in the life of the church. All these essential facts are provided in this second volume of these series of four books making up the exposition of the great subject of revival. Knowing these sound and cogent reasons behind God's revivals as well as the power of the Godhead and the power of the word of God behind all genuine revivals can go a long way to make our path clear, simple and straightforward towards the comprehension of God's spiritual revivals and spiritual renewals.

May the Lord God continue to use this second volume to guide us on this path of knowledge and to empower us and help us to receive and maintain His genuine and constant spiritual revivals and awakenings. In summary, read on to discover why we still need God's regular revivals in the Church of the Lord Jesus Christ today and how God the father, God the son, God the Holy Spirit and the unadulterated word of God can help us to receive God's revival fire and keep it burning all the time.

CHAPTER ONE

SOME HUMAN REASONS WHICH MAKE CONTINUOUS PERSONAL AND GROUP REVIVALS STILL NECESSARY IN THE CHURCH OF CHRIST TODAY

INTRODUCTION

There are several human reasons which make our need for God's constant revival, renewal, and restoration needful all the time both at the personal and general church levels. The source of all these human weaknesses can be traced to the disastrous effects of the Fall in the Garden of Eden. One of these unfortunate effects of the Fall is that as soon as it took place in the Garden of Eden, it predisposed all the descendants of Adam and Eve to continuous sinful weaknesses and sinful tendencies. So, even after our salvation when the power of sin becomes broken upon us, we are still capable of sinning though we are not prone to sin. This sinful inclination is described in Genesis 6:5 in the words:

"The Lord saw how great the wickedness of the human race had become on the earth, and that every inclination

of the thoughts of the human heart was only evil all the time." NIV

Because of this unfortunate human tendency, it would take only regular personal and group revivals in the church to keep us regularly strengthened to be able to press on in the Christian race in the power of the Holy Spirit. We want to discuss a few of these unfortunate human weaknesses and the advantages they sometimes offer Satan and his demons over us as proof of what we are saying here. The overall purpose of this chapter therefore is to goad us on to seek and pursue God's continuous revivals with all our strength to keep us going all the time. The details are presented in this chapter as follows:

<u>Bible Study and Personal Review Questions</u>
1. What human weakness in this chapter makes the need for regular revivals paramount in our lives?
2. When we trace its origin, what is the source of this unfortunate human weakness? (Genesis 6:5)
3. In what practical ways can regular revivals and spiritual renewals help us to bring this human weakness under the control of the Holy Spirit?

REGULAR PERSONAL AND GROUP REVIVALS ARE ALWAYS NEEDED IN THE CHURCH OF

CHRIST TODAY BECAUSE OF THE ERRATIC AND EVER-CHANGING NATURE OF MAN

Revivals in the church must never for any reasons be relegated to the pages of ancient history books. It will be a sad mistake for anyone to do this today. Because such an action will be failing to take cognisance of the fact that human nature has always been the same since the Fall of Adman and Eve as the first human beings in the Garden of Eden. *One of these dominant character weaknesses of Man since creation has always been our inability to stick to what is good for us permanently without faltering, wavering, going back and even sometimes falling totally.*

It is this character weakness in man which makes events like religious revivals necessary in the church at all times and throughout all the historical time periods up to our present day and even beyond until Christ comes to receive us into His glory. We see examples of this human character weakness surfacing in the lives of several Bible characters and groups of leaders including great saints of great faith as well as ordinary saints throughout the Old and New Testaments.

Because of this unfortunate human weakness, when we stop encouraging regular and constant personal and group revivals and other renewal programmes in the church, the church of the Lord Jesus Christ will soon become a decadent institution and lose its spiritual power and fervour. In this, it will become just like one of the ordinary social groups and institutions in the world with no spiritual cutting edge and effective spiritual ministry for the Lord Jesus Christ. This will in turn be detrimental to salvation and conversion and more seriously put millions of sincere Christians out of the Christian race and Christian journey altogether because of their continuous lukewarmness and spiritual coldness.

Some practical examples and exhibitions of some of these human weaknesses can be found in the lives of the following saints and body of believers to encourage us to seek God's continuous spiritual revival and renewal all the time:

1. King Solomon's Turn to Idolatry

<u>1 Kings 11:4</u>
As Solomon grew old, his wives turned his heart after other gods, and his heart was not fully devoted to the Lord his God, as the heart of David his father had been. NIV

<u>Deuteronomy 7:3-4</u>
Do not intermarry with them. Do not give your daughters to their sons or take their daughters for your sons, for they will turn your children away from following me to serve other gods, and the Lord's anger will burn against you and will quickly destroy you. NIV

2. Peter's Denial of Christ

Mark 14:66-72

While Peter was below in the courtyard, one of the servant girls of the high priest came by. When she saw Peter warming himself, she looked closely at him. "You also were with that Nazarene, Jesus," she said. But he denied it. "I don't know or understand what you're talking about," he said, and went out into the entryway. When the servant girl saw him there, she said again to those standing around, "This fellow is one of them." Again he denied it. After a little while, those standing near said to Peter, "Surely you are one of them, for you are a Galilean." He began to call down curses, and he swore to them, "I don't know this man you're talking about." Immediately the rooster crowed the second time. Then Peter remembered the word Jesus had spoken to him: "Before the rooster crows twice you will disown me three times." And he broke down and wept. NIV

Luke 22:61-62

And the Lord turned and looked at Peter. Then Peter remembered the word of the Lord, how He had said to him, "Before the rooster crows, you will deny Me three times." So Peter went out and wept bitterly. NKJV

John 21:15-17

So when they had eaten breakfast, Jesus said to Simon Peter, "Simon, son of Jonah, do you love Me more than these?" He said to Him, "Yes, Lord; You know that I love You." He said

to him, "Feed My lambs." He said to him again a second time, "Simon, son of Jonah, do you love Me?" He said to Him, "Yes, Lord; You know that I love You." He said to him, "Tend My sheep." He said to him the third time, "Simon, son of Jonah, do you love Me?" Peter was grieved because He said to him the third time, "Do you love Me?" And he said to Him, "Lord, You know all things; You know that I love You." Jesus said to him, "Feed My sheep. NKJV

Acts 3:14, 15

But you denied the Holy One and the Just, and asked for a murderer to be granted to you, and killed the Prince of life, whom God raised from the dead, of which we are witnesses. NKJV

3. Judas Iscariot's Betrayal

Matthew 26:14-16

Then one of the Twelve — the one called Judas Iscariot — went to the chief priests and asked, "What are you willing to give me if I deliver him over to you?" So they counted out for him thirty pieces of silver. From then on Judas watched for an opportunity to hand him over. NIV

John 13:21-26

After he had said this, Jesus was troubled in spirit and testified, "Very truly I tell you, one of you is going to betray me." His disciples stared at one another, at a loss to

know which of them he meant. One of them, the disciple whom Jesus loved, was reclining next to him. Simon Peter motioned to this disciple and said, "Ask him which one he means." Leaning back against Jesus, he asked him, "Lord, who is it?" Jesus answered, "It is the one to whom I will give this piece of bread when I have dipped it in the dish." Then, dipping the piece of bread, he gave it to Judas, the son of Simon Iscariot. NIV

Matthew 26:25
Then Judas, the one who would betray him, said, "Surely you don't mean me, Rabbi?" Jesus answered, "You have said so." NIV

4. Demas Abandoning Paul

Philemon 1:24
And so do Mark, Aristarchus, Demas and Luke, my fellow workers. NIV

2 Timothy 4:10
For Demas, because he loved this world, has deserted me and has gone to Thessalonica. Crescens has gone to Galatia, and Titus to Dalmatia. NIV

5. King Saul's Disobedience and Decline

1 Samuel 15:1-3
Samuel also said to Saul, "The Lord sent me to anoint you king over His people, over Israel. Now therefore, heed the

voice of the words of the Lord. Thus says the Lord of hosts: 'I will punish Amalek for what he did to Israel, how he ambushed him on the way when he came up from Egypt. Now go and attack Amalek, and utterly destroy all that they have, and do not spare them. But kill both man and woman, infant and nursing child, ox and sheep, camel and donkey.'" NKJV

<u>1 Samuel 15:9-11</u>
But Saul and the people spared Agag and the best of the sheep, the oxen, the fatlings, the lambs, and all that was good, and were unwilling to utterly destroy them. But everything despised and worthless, that they utterly destroyed. Now the word of the Lord came to Samuel, saying, "I greatly regret that I have set up Saul as king, for he has turned back from following Me, and has not performed My commandments." And it grieved Samuel, and he cried out to the Lord all night. NKJV

<u>1 Samuel 16:14</u>
Now the Spirit of the Lord had departed from Saul, and an evil spirit from the Lord tormented him. NIV

6. The Galatians' Return to Legalism

<u>Galatians 3:1-5</u>
You foolish Galatians! Who has bewitched you? Before your very eyes Jesus Christ was clearly portrayed as crucified. I would like to learn just one thing from you: Did you receive

the Spirit by the works of the law, or by believing what you heard? Are you so foolish? After beginning by means of the Spirit, are you now trying to finish by means of the flesh? Have you experienced so much in vain – if it really was in vain? So again I ask, does God give you his Spirit and work miracles among you by the works of the law, or by your believing what you heard? NIV

7. Lot in his wrongly choosing to go and live in Sodom

<u>Genesis 13:10-13</u>
And Lot lifted his eyes and saw all the plain of Jordan, that it was well watered everywhere (before the Lord destroyed Sodom and Gomorrah) like the garden of the Lord, like the land of Egypt as you go toward Zoar. Then Lot chose for himself all the plain of Jordan, and Lot journeyed east. And they separated from each other. Abram dwelt in the land of Canaan, and Lot dwelt in the cities of the plain and pitched his tent even as far as Sodom. But the men of Sodom were exceedingly wicked and sinful against the Lord. NKJV

<u>Genesis 19:1, 12, 13</u>
Now the two angels came to Sodom in the evening, and Lot was sitting in the gate of Sodom. When Lot saw them, he rose to meet them, and he bowed himself with his face toward the ground. Then the men said to Lot, "Have you anyone else here? Son-in-law, your sons, your daughters, and whomever you have in the city – take them out of this place! For we will

destroy this place, because the outcry against them has grown great before the face of the Lord, and the Lord has sent us to destroy it." NKJV

8. Samson in his wrongly choosing to marry Delilah

<u>Judges 14:1-3</u>

Now Samson went down to Timnah, and saw a woman in Timnah of the daughters of the Philistines. So he went up and told his father and mother, saying, "I have seen a woman in Timnah of the daughters of the Philistines; now therefore, get her for me as a wife." Then his father and mother said to him, "Is there no woman among the daughters of your brethren, or among all my people, that you must go and get a wife from the uncircumcised Philistines?" And Samson said to his father, "Get her for me, for she pleases me well." NKJV

<u>Judges 16:4-5, 18-20</u>

Afterward it happened that he loved a woman in the Valley of Sorek, whose name was Delilah. And the lords of the Philistines came up to her and said to her, "Entice him, and find out where his great strength lies, and by what means we may overpower him, that we may bind him to afflict him; and every one of us will give you eleven hundred pieces of silver." When Delilah saw that he had told her all his heart, she sent and called for the lords of the Philistines, saying, "Come up once more, for he has told me all his heart." So the lords of the Philistines came up to her and brought the money in their hand. Then she lulled him to sleep on her knees, and called for a man and had him shave off the seven locks of his head. Then she began to torment him, and his strength left him. And she said, "The Philistines are upon you, Samson!" So he awoke from his sleep, and said, "I will go out as before, at other times, and shake myself free!" But he did not know that the Lord had departed from him. NKJV

<u>Judges 16:28-31</u>
Then Samson called to the Lord, saying, "O Lord God, remember me, I pray! Strengthen me, I pray, just this once, O God, that I may with one blow take vengeance on the Philistines for my two eyes!" And Samson took hold of the two middle pillars which supported the temple, and he braced himself against them, one on his right and the other on his left. Then Samson said, "Let me die with the Philistines!" And he pushed with all his might, and the temple fell on the lords and all the people who were in it. So the dead that he killed at his death were more than he had killed in his life. And his brothers and all his father's household came down and took him, and brought him up and buried him between Zorah and Eshtaol in the tomb of his father Manoah. He had judged Israel twenty years. NKJV

9. King David in his sin with Bathsheba

<u>2 Samuel 11:1-5</u>

It happened in the spring of the year, at the time when kings go out to battle, that David sent Joab and his servants with him, and all Israel; and they destroyed the people of Ammon and besieged Rabbah. But David remained at Jerusalem. Then it happened one evening that David arose from his bed and walked on the roof of the king's house. And from the roof he saw a woman bathing, and the woman was very beautiful to behold. So David sent and inquired about the woman. And someone said, "Is this not Bathsheba, the daughter of Eliam, the wife of Uriah the Hittite?" Then David sent messengers, and took her; and she came to him, and he lay with her, for she was cleansed from her impurity; and she returned to her house. And the woman conceived; so she sent and told David, and said, "I am with child." NKJV

2 Samuel 12:7-9, 13

Then Nathan said to David, "You are the man! Thus says the Lord God of Israel: 'I anointed you king over Israel, and I delivered you from the hand of Saul. I gave you your master's house and your master's wives into your keeping, and gave you the house of Israel and Judah. And if that had been too little, I also would have given you much more! Why have you despised the commandment of the Lord, to do evil in His sight? You have killed Uriah the Hittite with the sword; you have taken his wife to be your wife, and have killed him with the sword of the people of Ammon. So David said to Nathan, "I have sinned against the Lord." And

Nathan said to David, "The Lord also has put away your sin; you shall not die. NKJV

10. The Ephesian Church in forgetting its first love

Revelation 2:4-5

Nevertheless I have this against you, that you have left your first love. Remember therefore from where you have fallen; repent and do the first works, or else I will come to you quickly and remove your lampstand from its place — unless you repent. NKJV

All the numerous references quoted above are graphic illustrations of the erratic and ever-changing nature of man. They all knew what was good and constituted God's perfect will yet they moved away from them. It only took God's grace and spiritual restoration to keep them going. It is this unfortunate nature of man which makes regular spiritual revivals, renewals and restorations still indispensable in the church of the Lord Jesus Christ. It is to help us to avoid similar unfortunate incidents that we need God's regular personal and group revivals to get the necessary spiritual renewal, power and strength to be able to press on even when the going becomes tough and the spiritual road becomes rough and impassable. Let us now move on to the second main reason which also emphasizes our need for God's constant revivals in the Church of Christ today.

Bible Study and Personal Review Questions

1. What one dominant human weakness is mentioned here as one of the main reasons for regular revivals in the church?
2. When it is allowed to work freely in believers in the Church of Christ, what can be some of its disastrous effects in the Church?
3. Go through the 10 manifestations of this human weakness in the lives of the saints concerned and answer the following search questions on each of the personalities or groups:
   a. What is the name or identification of the person in question?
   b. What can you say about his/her former commitment and dedication to God?
   c. How did this unfortunate human weakness come into his/her life to derail him/her?
   d. Why did they falter considering the fact that initially they were absolutely faithful to God? Did they not know the right thing to do at the time they were tempted?
   e. What do you think caused them to fail God at this critical time?

f. What were the results of their failure?

g. What did God do to help them to be able to continue to walk with Him?

h. What lessons can we learn from each of them on the need for God's regular revivals to get renewed spiritual strength and empowerment as we also continue to walk with God in the Church of Christ?

WE NEED CONSTANT PERSONAL AND GROUP REVIVALS BECAUSE OF SATAN'S WICKED INTENTIONS FOR US AS INDIVIDUAL CHRISTIANS AND AS A CHURCH

One other major reason which makes our search for God's daily revivals as Christians a continuous divine imperative is Satan's wicked intentions for us as God's true children and as the faithful followers of Christ. What are some of these evil motives of Satan and his wicked accomplices? Some of them can be read from the scriptures as follows:

<u>1 Peter 5:8</u>
Be alert and of sober mind. Your enemy the devil prowls around like a roaring lion looking for someone to devour. NIV

<u>Job 2:2</u>
And the Lord said to Satan, "Where have you come from?" Satan answered the Lord, "From roaming

<u>Revelation 12:9</u>
The great dragon was hurled down — that ancient serpent called the devil, or Satan, who leads the whole world astray. He was hurled to the earth, and his angels with him. NIV

According to the few references quoted above, what are Satan's intentions for all the true children of God and for all the forces of good in the world in general? All the three references first emphasize Satan's interminable itinerary and movements in the world. 1 Peter 5:8 states it in the words, "who prowls around." Satan himself confesses and confirms this in Job 2:2 in the words, "from roaming throughout the earth, going back and forth on it." Revelation 12:9 also emphasizes this with the scope of Satan's wicked ministry in the words: "who leads the whole world astray." What is Satan's chief motive for moving around everywhere in the world all the time? Is it to do good and display acts of benevolence? This is never the case because 1 Peter 5:8 states the purpose of his movements as being mainly destructive. It states that the devil moves around "seeking whom he may devour." So it can be asserted that his purpose of going to that place where righteous Job was was also to seek and explore opportunities to destroy him.

The second reason for Satan's movement around the world is given to us in the passage quoted from Revelation 12:9 in the words, "who leads the whole world astray." If as Christians we have an enemy who is as wicked and destructive as Satan, then should we neglect God's regular revivals which can give us regular spiritual renewals and empowerment to be able to stand against him? As stated in the few instances quoted above, his main purpose of perambulating the earth and moving about everywhere in the world is to seek opportunity to unleash vicious spiritual attacks to cause spiritual instability and spiritual destruction to further his aim of stealing, killing and destroying as it is stated in John 10:10 in the words: "The thief does not come except to steal, and to kill, and to destroy. I have come that they may have life, and that they may have it more abundantly."

In all the passages quoted under the erratic nature of man at the beginning of this chapter, Satan and his adversaries got the chance to tempt and destabilize all these great saints because of the spiritual weakness which came into their lives at the time of his attacks. So we can say that the devil attacked them at the time they were both spiritually and physically vulnerable. We are not better than them in any way because initially, some of them were even capable of calling down God's fire directly from heaven to consume their sacrifices.

So the truths and practical lessons we can learn from them and from Satan's endless wicked roamings is that we always need to be on fire for God through constant spiritual revivals and renewals to be able to overcome all the wiles of Satan and his demons and keep them away from us and from our path. And how can we continually be on fire for God this way if we do not check ourselves with God's word, repent and confess where necessary and pray for his revival, renewal and spiritual constancy?

Satan is not indomitable. He and his adversaries can always be conquered and defeated in the name of the Lord Jesus Christ by Christians who are spiritually active and vibrant through regular personal and group revivals to be able to apply James 4:7 successfully in all spiritual encounters. Let us at this juncture examine other scriptural passages like James 4:7 which assure us that when we always remain aglow in the Spirit through personal and group revivals, we can successfully resist and defeat Satan and his demons in the name of the Lord Jesus Christ and in the strength and power of the Holy Spirit:

> James 4:7
> *Submit yourselves, then, to God. Resist the devil,*
> *and he will flee from you.* NIV

> Ephesians 4:27
> *And do not give the devil a foothold.* NIV

<u>1 Peter 5:9</u>
Resist him, standing firm in the faith, because you know that the family of believers throughout the world is undergoing the same kind of sufferings.
NIV

Although all the passages quoted above do emphasize that it is possible to resist Satan and be effectual in doing this, it should be quickly added that resisting Satan successfully can never be done in the flesh with spiritual weakness. This can be inferred from the meaning of the word "Resist" which means to repel something coming against you with some power and strength which is greater and far in excess of what is coming against you. So nobody can successfully resist Satan and his demons with spiritual weakness due to lack of regular revivals, renewals, restorations and spiritual empowerment. It is in this vein that Merriam-Webster's dictionary gives the following two different definitions of the word "Resist". It defines it as follows:

1. To exert force in opposition.
2. To exert oneself so as to counteract or defeat.

Though it has become clear from our discussion, we still want to reemphasize that one major reason for Satan moving around every day, everywhere in the world is to seek opportunities to destroy us as believers and God's children. He works everywhere like a roaring lion seeking whom he may devour. He moves around as the tempter who sets traps and snares for our feet. Even in ordinary life situations, if you are told that some enemies are around you and are hiding in a secret place because of you, is this the time to sleep, relax, become careless and become spiritually negligent? Rather is it not the time to maintain your strength and engage in practical activities which can put you in top form to be able to protect yourself and overpower such enemies with ease?

Revival is the spiritual exercise which when sought regularly both personally and at the general church level, can strengthen, renew, restore and empower us to be able to resist and face the devil and all our enemies successfully; and further pave the way for God to ward off all the attacks emanating from their evil camp towards us. It is for this reason that the Bible encourages us to constantly stay revived to be able to apply the scriptures on successful resistance and stand against the devil and his hordes of demons and evil spirits.

Apart from Satan's evil and wicked activities against us as individual Christians, he always harbours evil intentions against the church of the Lord Jesus Christ also. This is not surprising because every true believer is also part of this universal church of Christ. Some of his evil intentions against the Church can be summed up as follows:

SOME OF SATAN'S EVIL PLANS AND ACTIVITIES AGAINST THE CHURCH AND ITS BELIEVERS

1. Satan works to blind the minds of unbelievers so that they will never heed to the message of the gospel.
   2 Corinthians 4:4
   Whose minds the god of this age has blinded, who do not believe, lest the light of the gospel of the glory of Christ, who is the image of God, should shine on them. NKJV

2. Satan is a liar and the father of all liars so he is always at work to cause people to believe his lies rather than the true gospel.
   John 8:44
   You are of your father the devil, and the desires of your father you want to do. He was a murderer from the beginning, and does not stand in the truth, because there is no truth in him. When he speaks a lie, he speaks from his own resources, for he is a liar and the father of it. NKJV

3. Satan works as a deceiver who sometimes parades as an agent of righteousness by transforming himself into an angel of light.
   2 Corinthians 11:14
   And no wonder! For Satan himself transforms himself into an angel of light. NKJV

4. In this end-time period, Satan can deceive with lying wonders, signs and false miracles.
   2 Thessalonians 2:9

The coming of the lawless one is according to the working of Satan, with all power, signs, and lying wonders. NKJV

5. Satan is a tempter who always works to tempt genuine children of God to sin.

    Mark 1:13

    And He was there in the wilderness forty days, tempted by Satan, and was with the wild beasts; and the angels ministered to Him. NKJV

6. Satan works to steal the seed of the genuine word of God out of people's hearts.

    Luke 8:11-12

    "Now the parable is this: The seed is the word of God. Those by the wayside are the ones who hear; then the devil comes and takes away the word out of their hearts, lest they should believe and be saved. NKJV

7. Satan works to choke the growing faith of genuine believers.

    Luke 8:14

    Now the ones that fell among thorns are those who, when they have heard, go out and are choked with cares, riches, and pleasures of life, and bring no fruit to maturity. NKJV

8. In extreme cases, Satan can inflict sicknesses and diseases upon innocent people.

    Job 2:7

    So Satan went out from the presence of the Lord, and struck Job with painful boils from the sole of his foot to the crown of his head. NKJV

<u>Mark 1:32-34</u>

At evening, when the sun had set, they brought to Him all who were sick and those who were demon-possessed. And the whole city was gathered together at the door. Then He healed many who were sick with various diseases, and cast out many demons; and He did not allow the demons to speak, because they knew Him. NKJV

9. Satan can sometimes work to try to hinder the spread of the gospel and missions effort.

<u>1 Thessalonians 2:18</u>

Therefore we wanted to come to you — even I, Paul, time and again — but Satan hindered us. NKJV

10. Satan is an accuser who accuses Christians before God to draw them into discouragement.

<u>Revelation 12:10</u>

Then I heard a loud voice saying in heaven, "Now salvation, and strength, and the kingdom of our God, and the power of His Christ have come, for the accuser of our brethren, who accused them before our God day and night, has been cast down. NKJV

11. But Satan is already a defeated foe in the mighty name of the Lord Jesus Christ.

<u>1 John 3:8</u>

He who sins is of the devil, for the devil has sinned from the beginning. For this purpose the Son of God was manifested, that He might destroy the works of the devil. NKJV

<u>Romans 16:20</u>
And the God of peace will crush Satan under your feet shortly. The grace of our Lord Jesus Christ be with you. Amen. NKJV

When God gave birth to the Church through the ministry of the Lord Jesus Christ, He had good plans for it. The first among these reasons was the task given to the church to get involved in missions throughout its existence on earth to be able to work to fulfil the Great Commission. A second major function given to the church in addition to this task was the provision of continuous fellowship to be able to nurture God's people to grow steadily without falling as we read in Bible passages like Acts 2:42, Ephesians 4:16, Hebrews 10:25 and Ephesians 5:19.

<u>Acts 2:42</u>
They devoted themselves to the apostles' teaching and to fellowship, to the breaking of bread and to prayer. NIV

<u>Ephesians 4:16</u>
From him the whole body, joined and held together by every supporting ligament, grows and builds itself up in love, as each part does its work. NIV

<u>Hebrews 10:25</u>

Not giving up meeting together, as some are in the habit of doing, but encouraging one another – and all the more as you see the Day approaching. NIV

<u>Ephesians 5:19</u>
Speaking to one another with psalms, hymns, and songs from the Spirit. Sing and make music from your heart to the Lord. NIV

But these are two of the major ministries of the church which Satan and His evil collaborators are always working hard to fight against and to destroy as Christ emphasized in the parable of the wheat and tares on the work of the kingdom of God (Matthew 13:24-30).

In His interpretation of this parable, this was what Christ had to say about the tares and the devil who sowed them: "He answered, "The one who sowed the good seed is the Son of Man. The field is the world, and the good seed stands for the people of the kingdom. The weeds are the people of the evil one, and the enemy who sows them is the devil. The harvest is the end of the age, and the harvesters are angels." (Matthew 13:37-39). For this and many other reasons, we need regular revivals and renewals in the church to be able to get the needed strength and power to destroy and set aside all the satanic oppositions to the noble God-given tasks in the church.

The good news for us as true children of God is that the Lord Jesus and the Holy Spirit are actively working in the church to provide us with the needed power and anointing to be able to defeat Satan totally and constantly for the work of the church to go on unhindered. As we have already learnt, resisting Satan as truly revived children of God can always be successful because Satan has great limitations which make him powerless against genuinely born-again Spirit-filled Christians who are burning with the fire of the Holy Spirit.

These limitations include the fact that, 1. Satan is not omnipotent like the mighty God, 2. Satan is not omnipresent like the mighty God, 3. Satan is not omniscient like the mighty God, 4. Satan is not eternal like the mighty God, 5. Though Satan is a spirit, he was only created as an angel of God so resisting him with the power of the genuine Holy Spirit of God in the mighty name of the Lord Jesus and in the light of Scriptures like James 4:7 which reads: "Therefore submit to God. Resist the devil and he will flee from you," can always be effectual to enable both the church and the individual saints of Christ forge ahead in continuous spiritual victory.

Bible Study and Personal Review Questions

1. Who is the devil? What is his origin?
2. If the devil is an angel then why is he not serving in God's presence in heaven like all the holy angels?
3. What are the aims of Satan and his fallen angels as they move round everywhere in the world?
4. When we bring this truth further down, what are some of the evil intentions of Satan and his fallen angels against you as a faithful and true child of God?
5. What is the biblical way of dealing with Satan and his demons to prevent them from gaining any spiritual or practical advantage over us?
6. Can this work of resisting Satan and his demons successfully be done in the power of the flesh?
7. How can regular revivals, renewals and restorations help us to do this successfully all the time?
8. What is involved in saying that you are going to reisist the devil? Can a lesser power resist a greater power?
9. If the answer to the above question is no, then how can regular revivals, renewals and restorations accompanied by the release of God's great power help us in this enterprise.
10. What are the two major ministries given to the worldwide church by Christ?

11. What are some of the evil activities of the devil against these important activities of the Church?

12. When we pick and analyze these evil activities one by one, what are some of the evils they can bring into the church if they are left unchecked?

13. What are some of the theological facts which make our resisting the devil as genuine Christians always possible?

WE NEED GOD'S CONSTANT PERSONAL AND GROUP REVIVALS BECAUSE REVIVALS HAVE ALWAYS BEEN GOD'S PRINCIPAL MEANS OF RESTORATION AFTER PERIODS OF SERIOUS SPIRITUAL DECLINE IN THE BIBLE

In this end-time period which is characterized by sin, wickedness and spiritual deception, taking revivals out of the church as the body of believers and out of our personal lives as the individual members of the body of Christ can be spiritually disastrous and degenerating. This will be comparable to taking the sun around which all the planets in our solar system revolve out of our present solar system and still expecting light to shine on earth every day as well as on all the other planets. This will be totally impossible because the sun is the great source of the light!

What we are trying to emphasize with this comparison is that in God's dealings with His people in the Old Testament, in the New Testament and all through the history of the church up to the present day, revivals and regular spiritual renewals leading to restoration have always been God's great strategy of bringing His people back to Himself after periods of serious spiritual decline and total spiritual backsliding and backwardness. There is ample proof from the scriptures and other reliable historical sources for this claim. Let us start by examining some of these proofs from the Old Testament by quoting from Walter Kaiser's book bearing the title "Quest for Renewal". It has this important observation to make about serious spiritual declines and their connection with God's revivals, renewals and restorations:

> *"Most revivals were preceded by a time of deep spiritual decline and despair. For example, there was the Egyptian bondage, which led to the golden calf debacle, or the time prior to the revival under King Hezekiah, which involved the revolting practice of offering children as burnt offerings on the altar of Molech. No different was the situation in Elijah's time, with the maddening spectacle of a whole nation gathering on Mount Carmel, unable to decide whether to worship Baal or Yahweh. All were times of deep spiritual decline, and they match our own in many ways."*

This quotation must be understood from these two angles. First, spiritual declines though not desired can affect God's people from time to time. Secondly, whenever such spiritual declines occur, God out of His love and concern always uses revivals, renewals and restorations to bring great interventions in the spiritual decline so as to be able to bring His people back to Himself. As proof of this, we want to discuss some of the instances mentioned in the quotation above together with some other general ones as follows:

SOME INSTANCES IN THE LIFE OF THE CHILDREN OF ISRAEL IN GENERAL

Exodus 32:1-6

Now when the people saw that Moses delayed coming down from the mountain, the people gathered together to Aaron, and said to him, "Come, make us gods that shall go before us; for as for this Moses, the man who brought us up out of the land of Egypt, we do not know what has become of him." And Aaron said to them, "Break off the golden earrings which are in the ears of your wives, your sons, and your daughters, and bring them to me." So all the people broke off the golden earrings which were in their ears, and brought them to Aaron. And he received the gold from their hand, and he fashioned it with an engraving tool, and made a molded calf. Then they said, "This is your god, O Israel, that brought you out of the land of Egypt!" So when Aaron saw it, he built an altar before it. And Aaron made a proclamation and said, "Tomorrow is a feast to the Lord." Then they rose early on the next day, offered burnt offerings, and brought peace offerings; and the people sat down to eat and drink, and rose up to play. NKJV

Exodus 32:11-14

Then Moses pleaded with the Lord his God, and said: "Lord, why does Your wrath burn hot against Your people whom You have brought out of the land of Egypt with great power and with a mighty hand? Why should the Egyptians speak, and say, 'He brought them out to harm them, to kill them in the mountains, and to consume them from the face of the earth'? Turn from Your fierce wrath, and relent from this harm to Your people. Remember Abraham, Isaac, and Israel, Your servants, to whom You swore by Your own self, and said to them, I will multiply your descendants as the stars of heaven; and all this land that I have spoken of I give to your descendants, and they shall inherit it forever.'" So the Lord relented from the harm which He said He would do to His people. NKJV

Exodus 32:30-34

Now it came to pass on the next day that Moses said to the people, "You have committed a great sin. So now I will go up to the Lord; perhaps I can make atonement for your sin." Then Moses returned to the Lord and said, "Oh, these people have committed a great sin, and have made for themselves a god of gold! Yet now, if You will forgive their sin — but if not, I pray, blot me out of Your book which You have written." And the Lord said to Moses, "Whoever has sinned against Me, I will blot him out of My book. Now therefore, go, lead the people to the place of which I have spoken to you. Behold, My Angel shall go before you. Nevertheless, in the day when I visit for punishment, I will visit punishment upon them for their sin." NKJV

In Israel's journey from Egypt to the promised land, one dominant characteristic we observe is Israel's disobedience to God coupled with their murmuring and sometimes even open rebellion. What brought Israel to the promised land was therefore God's grace which always cured the Israelites of these unfortunate sins and brought them repentance and restoration to be able to continue with their journey until they reached the promised land. An instance is the worship of the golden calf which Aaron made for them when Moses went up to the mountain to meet God. In all these episodes we see three major elements of revival which manifest as follows:

First, the spiritual declension calling for revival always begins with sin on the part of Israel. This makes them guilty before God and naturally brings down God's wrath upon them. The same trend exists in the church today. Sin always destroys God's power, presence and favour in the church. The second element always involves repentance and restitution. Because God is forever holy and can never tolerate sin, when His people sin, He naturally rebukes them to draw their attention to this unfortunate spiritual failure. This then brings the intermission and intercession of his leaders like Moses and others to lead the people into practical repentance and confession.

Finally, out of His mercy and grace, God forgives His people, brings them restoration and renewal and restores His fellowship with them. This is a clear picture of how God walks with His people. Because we are sometimes inclined to sin and waywardness as a result of the Fall, when God takes revivals and periods of restoration out of the church, there is no way we can guarantee that everybody will finish the Christian race successfully without any sinful spots. Just as He used these same revivals and periods of renewal and restoration in His walk with Israel as a nation, so does He still use these same spiritual principles of repentance, revivals, renewals and restorations to help us in our walk with Him in the church. The passages quoted and discussed above give clear proof of what we are saying. Other biblical episodes which can be quoted as further proofs of this assertion can be discussed as follows:

IN THE MINISTRY OF THE PROPHET ELIJAH
<u>1 Kings 18:22-24</u>
Then Elijah said to the people, "I alone am left a prophet of the Lord; but Baal's prophets are four hundred and fifty men. Therefore let them give us two bulls; and let them choose one bull for themselves, cut it in pieces, and lay it on the wood, but put no fire under it; and I will prepare the other bull, and lay it on the wood, but put no fire under it. Then you call on the name of your gods, and I will call on the name of the Lord; and the God who answers by fire, He is God." So all the people answered and said, "It is well spoken." NKJV

<u>1 Kings 18:26, 28, 29</u>
So they took the bull which was given them, and they prepared it, and called on the name of Baal from morning even till noon, saying, "O Baal, hear us!" But there was no voice; no one answered. Then they leaped about the altar which they had made. So they cried aloud, and cut themselves, as was their custom, with knives and lances, until the blood gushed out on them. And when midday was past, they prophesied until the time of the offering of the evening sacrifice. But there was no voice; no one answered, no one paid attention. NKJV

<u>1 Kings 18:36-38</u>

A very sad period in the history of Israel was the time when the whole nation became idolatrous, and Baal worship became the order of the day. Through state promotion by the King of Israel and his idolatrous wife, Israel forsook their holy God and replaced Him with idol worship. When God wanted to change this trend to bring His people back to Himself, what did He do? He brought in a mighty period of revival and restoration through the ministry of the prophet Elijah which reestablished and reemphasized that the worship of idols was useless and it was only the worship of Jehovah God which was sane, sensible and worthwhile as we read from the passages quoted above. This is another major proof of the claim that revivals are always needed in the church and will forever be needed in the church because they have always been God's major means of restoring His people back to Himself anytime they go wayward and forsake Him and His covenant.

ADDITIONAL PROOFS OF REVIVALS AND RESTORATIONS AFTER BACKSLIDING

Additional proofs for what we are discussing in this section about God's use of revivals and special times of restoration to bring His people back to Himself anytime they backslide can be obtained from an examination of the following biblical passages which also deal with periods of spiritual declension in Israel and God's subsequent restoration through His grace and mercy:

AHAZ

<u>2 Kings 16:2-4</u>
Ahaz was twenty years old when he became king, and he reigned sixteen years in Jerusalem; and he did not do what was right in the sight of the Lord his God, as his father David had done. But he walked in the way of the kings of Israel; indeed he made his son pass through the fire, according to the abominations of the nations whom the Lord had cast out from before the children of Israel. And he sacrificed and burned incense on the high places, on the hills, and under every green tree. NKJV

HEZEKIAH

<u>2 Kings 18:5-8</u>

He trusted in the Lord God of Israel, so that after him was none like him among all the kings of Judah, nor who were before him. For he held fast to the Lord; he did not depart from following Him, but kept His commandments, which the Lord had commanded Moses. The Lord was with him; he prospered wherever he went. And he rebelled against the king of Assyria and did not serve him. He subdued the Philistines, as far as Gaza and its territory, from watchtower to fortified city. NKJV

MANASSEH

<u>2 Chronicles 33:1-4</u>

Manasseh was twelve years old when he became king, and he reigned fifty-five years in Jerusalem. But he did evil in the sight of the Lord, according to the abominations of the nations whom the Lord had cast out before the children of Israel. For he rebuilt the high places which Hezekiah his father had broken down; he raised up altars for the Baals, and made wooden images; and he worshiped all the host of heaven and served them. He also built altars in the house of the Lord, of which the Lord had said, "In Jerusalem shall My name be forever." NKJV

<u>2 Chronicles 33:10-13, 15, 16</u>

And the Lord spoke to Manasseh and his people, but they would not listen. Therefore the Lord brought upon them the captains of the army of the king of Assyria, who took Manasseh with hooks, bound him with bronze fetters, and carried him off to Babylon.

Now when he was in affliction, he implored the Lord his God, and humbled himself greatly before the God of his fathers, and prayed to Him; and He received his entreaty, heard his supplication, and brought him back to Jerusalem into his kingdom. Then Manasseh knew that the Lord was God. He took away the foreign gods and the idol from the house of the Lord, and all the altars that he had built in the mount of the house of the Lord and in Jerusalem; and he cast them out of the city. He also repaired the altar of the Lord, sacrificed peace offerings and thank offerings on it, and commanded Judah to serve the Lord God of Israel. NKJV

AMON

<u>2 Chronicles 33:21-23</u>
Amon was twenty-two years old when he became king, and he reigned two years in Jerusalem. But he did evil in the sight of the Lord, as his father Manasseh had done; for Amon sacrificed to all the carved images which his father Manasseh had made, and served them. And he did not humble himself before the Lord, as his father Manasseh had humbled himself; but Amon trespassed more and more. NKJV

JOSIAH

<u>2 Chronicles 34:3-5</u>
For in the eighth year of his reign, while he was still young, he began to seek the God of his father David; and in the twelfth year

he began to purge Judah and Jerusalem of the high places, the wooden images, the carved images, and the molded images. They broke down the altars of the Baals in his presence, and the incense altars which were above them he cut down; and the wooden images, the carved images, and the molded images he broke in pieces, and made dust of them and scattered it on the graves of those who had sacrificed to them. He also burned the bones of the priests on their altars, and cleansed Judah and Jerusalem. NKJV

Bible Study and Personal Review Questions

1. Why are we saying that doing away with personal and group revivals in the Church can be both disastrous and degenerating?
2. What comparisons do we have in Astrology to prove this claim?
3. What are some of the historical episodes which can be used to prove this claim during the period of the exodus?
4. What further proofs can we get for this during the time of great prophets like Elijah? What additional proofs can we get for this during the reign of kings like Ahaz, Hezekiah, Manasseh, Amon and Josiah?
5. What great lesson should we learn from all these numerous instances of backslidings and restorations in connection with our seeking God's personal revivals

and corporate revivals involving all the members of the local church with constancy?

With this in view, what do you think can happen spiritually to a local church which has no regular revival and renewal programmes to help its members? What are some of the unfortunate sins and evil tendencies which can become prevalent in such a church?

CHAPTER TWO

SOME PRACTICAL AND THEOLOGICAL REASONS WHICH MAKE CONTINUOUS PERSONAL AND GROUP REVIVALS STILL NECESSARY IN THE CHURCH OF CHRIST TODAY

<u>INTRODUCTION</u>

Regular revivals in the Church of Christ are still needed today as they were needed in all periods of spiritual decline throughout the Holy Scriptures. Today there are several practical and theological reasons which make God's revivals indispensable in the spiritual life of the Church. All through church history, it is the eternal Holy Spirit who has been working in all the ministries of the church including bringing spiritual renewals to the faithful children of God. So we also need His ministry of regular spiritual revival and spiritual rejuvenation in this end-time period also called the dispensation of grace.

One great spiritual truth about the ministry of the Holy Spirit which we can deduce from all that we have been saying is that He has always been the great power behind all revivals and religious renewals by encouraging and promoting hatred for sin and great love for and commitment to God's righteous standards. One way He has been doing this is through periodic revivals, spiritual renewals and spiritual restoration programmes. It is for this reason that in this chapter, we want to present some cogent reasons which make the need for continuous revivals and other spiritual renewal programmes more urgent in the Church today than in any other period in church history.

Specifically, we want to establish as the number one reason that, we need regular revivals in the church to enable it work towards the fulfilment of its three-fold mission on earth. Secondly, we need regular revivals in the church to enable it nurture and prepare God's people and make them ready for the rapture. So Holy Ghost revivals are a must everywhere in the Church today. Let us now start dealing with the reasons one by one starting with the three-fold mission of the church on earth.

REVIVALS AND THE FULFILMENT OF THE THREE-FOLD MISSION OF THE CHURCH ON EARTH
We want to state here in plain language that the Church of the Lord Jesus Christ has been given a three-fold mission and ministry to fulfil for God on earth as it waits for the rapture. First, it has a divine mission to fulfil towards God. Secondly, it has a divine mission to fulfil towards itself.

Thirdly, it has a divine mission to fulfil towards the world. It can be stated without any fear of contradiction that none of these God-given objectives can be fulfilled in an atmosphere of spiritual coldness, spiritual declension and total spiritual lukewarmness. So this places an unavoidable obligation upon the faithful church of the Lord Jesus Christ to keep the Church at all its levels – local, national and international – fully revived at all times to be able to nurture its members and empower them regularly for optimum performance as it seeks to fulfil this three-fold mission on earth.

It must be reemphasized here that it is only in an atmosphere of regular revival, renewal and restoration that the Church can work to fulfil this three-fold mandate given by God with success because they are all great spiritual responsibilities. Therefore, if the Church is allowed to descend into any state of permanent spiritual coldness, this vision and mandate given by the triune God can never be fulfilled! Let us now take this three-fold responsibility of the Church one by one and discuss all the details involved in each of them which when strictly observed in this atmosphere of revival we are talking about can bring great success to the church. What is the first part of this three-fold mission given to the church? It can be stated this way:

Bible Study and Personal Review Questions

1. What do we understand today as the three-fold mission and mandate of the church of Christ?
2. Why is this three-fold responsibility often described as a mandate?
3. Is it valid to claim that this three-fold mandate can only be fulfilled in an atmosphere of revival?

THE CHURCH HAS A DIVINE RESPONSIBILITY TOWARDS GOD

What is this divine mandate which the church has to strive to fulfil towards God? Of a truth, the church's divine mandate towards God embraces all the things the church is supposed to do for God whiles on earth. But because none of these activities can be done successfully for God without the constant manifestation of His full presence and power, we want to sum everything up under this sub-topic by exploring some effective ways we can always seek, obtain and maintain God's powerful presence and omnipotent power in the church all the time. This is necessary because before the church can do anything practically to fulfill its numerous responsibilities towards God, it needs this spiritual aura which combines God's presence and power to be able to function and perform. Let us now go into the specifics of receiving and maintaining God's presence and power on a permanent basis in the church under the following sub-topics:

Bible Study and Personal Review Questions
1. What has God's presence and power got to do with the fulfilment of the three-fold mandate of the church on earth?
2. Is there anything the Church is supposed to do on earth for God which cannot be considered as part of this three-fold mandate?
3. What is the importance of God's permanent presence and power to our being able to do anything for Him until the rapture?

THE DEFINITION AND EXPLANATION OF GOD'S PRESENCE

What exactly can be described as God's presence? **God's special presence is anywhere He chooses to be or to dwell in a special way with His mighty power because the appropriate spiritual conditions have been provided to enable Him to do this as a holy God.**

To understand God's presence fully, it is important at this juncture to explain the three major ways God's presence can be felt in the church and generally everywhere. God's presence can first be felt and experienced in His **omnipresence.** God has filled the whole of His creation and His full presence is felt everywhere and in every part of His creation at the same time. So before God created human beings on earth, His presence could be felt everywhere. His omnipresence fills the church, fills our home, fills space, fills heaven and fills every corner of the earth. Consequently, we do not need to pray or do anything special to be able to receive God's omnipresence in His church. References on God's omnipresence can be read as follows:

<u>Job 34:21</u>
For His eyes are on the ways of man, and He sees all his steps. NKJV

<u>Proverbs 15:3</u>
The eyes of the Lord are in every place, keeping watch on the evil and the good. NKJV

<u>Jeremiah 23:24</u>
Can anyone hide himself in secret places, so I shall not see him?" says the Lord; "Do I not fill heaven and earth?" says the Lord. NKJV

<u>Psalm 139:7-10</u>
Where can I go from Your Spirit? or where can I flee from Your presence? If I ascend into heaven, You are there; if I make my bed in hell, behold, You are there. If I take the wings of the morning, and dwell in the uttermost parts of the sea, even there Your

*hand shall lead me, and Your right hand shall hold
me.* NKJV

Hebrews 4:13
*And there is no creature hidden from His sight, but
all things are naked and open to the eyes of Him to
whom we must give account.* NKJV

The second level of God's presence is His **personal
presence** with His people. When we come to accept the
Lord Jesus Christ as our personal saviour and start living
for Him faithfully in holiness and purity, the triune God
comes to dwell in us as John 14:23 says in the words: *"Jesus
answered and said to him, "If anyone loves Me, he will keep My
word; and My Father will love him, and We will come to him
and make Our home with him.""* NKJV. Because of this
unique spiritual experience, the Bible describes us as
temples of the Holy Spirit, that is, temples in which the
Holy Spirit is dwelling permanently as we read from 1
Corinthians 6:19 in the words *"Or do you not know that your
body is the temple of the Holy Spirit who is in you, whom you
have from God, and you are not your own?"* NKJV

This is the reason why we are able to experience personal
revivals as individual Christians wherever we are when
we fulfil the necessary spiritual conditions attached to this
experience. It is this personal presence of God which also
makes Matthew 18:20 possible in family prayers and in the

prayers of small groups and fellowships of believers. It reads as follows: *"For where two or three are gathered together in My name, I am there in the midst of them."* NKJV

The third level of God's presence is His **manifest presence.** God's manifest presence is His special presence which whenever and wherever it is revealed is always accompanied by some physical signs and physical manifestations as proof of God's mighty presence with His people. The Cambridge dictionary defines manifest as an act which shows something clearly through signs or actions.

There are several examples of God's manifest presence in the Bible. On the Day of Pentecost, God's manifest presence were the rushing mighty wind and tongues of fire (Acts 2:1-3). In the Exodus, God's manifest presence were the pillar of cloud by day and the pillar of fire by night (Exodus 13:21). In the tabernacle, God's manifest presence was on the mercy seat between the two Cherubim (Exodus 25:19, 21a, 22). In coming down to call Moses, God's manifest presence was the burning bush which was not consumed (Exodus 3:2-6). God's manifest presence on Mount Sanai to show Israel who He was. He came with thunder, lightning, fire and smoke (Exodus 19:16-18).

God's manifest presence to the prophet Elijah in the wilderness included strong wind, an earthquake a fire and a still small voice (1 Kings 19:9-12). At the dedication of Solomon's temple, God's manifest presence came down in the form of fire and His glory filling the temple. (2 Chronicles 7:1). Finally on the Mount of Transfiguration, God's manifest presence came down in the form of His special glory together with the message, *"This is My beloved Son. Hear Him!"* (Luke 9:29-35)

How can we also experience God's manifest presence in the church today as we pray, worship, seek God's revival and renewal and seek God's divine power? While we cannot say that our experience should exactly be like those cited above, there could be some modern versions as follows:

Depending on the personalities concerned there can be different manifestations to indicate God's special presence. These manifestations can include shaking, inability to stand still, kneeling, shedding of tears, lying prostrate on the bare floor, special inspiration to prophetic utterances and so on. One general truth about all these manifestations is that because they all occur under the direct control of the Holy Spirit, they are neither aggressive nor harmful to anybody. But they all occur to bring glory to God.

CONCLUSION

Now the question arises again. As we seek to maintain God's presence in the church, which of these three levels of God's presence should we place the emphasis on? His omnipresence was in the church before we entered it. We came into the church that day with His personal presence which is always with us wherever we go as long as we remain His genuine children. What we do not always have is God's manifest presence which always comes into the church through revivals and other spiritual renewal programmes with great power and the powerful hand of God as it occurred in the early church on the Day of Pentecost. So let us always pray for this level of God's power which is special and can always bring God's manifest presence to empower and elevate us spiritually. If we do this regularly, God's special presence and mighty power will always stay in His church to help us fulfil our responsibilities towards Him as a universal church.

Bible Study and Personal Review Questions
1. What exactly can be described as God's presence in the church? In connection with this how can we define God's presence?
2. What is God's omnipresence? Where and how do we experience this omnipresence of God?

3. What is God's personal presence? Who are those who qualify to receive God's personal presence and by what means?
4. What is God's manifest presence? Why is it called a "manifest presence"?
5. What are some of the examples of God's manifest presence in the Bible?
6. What type and level of God's presence should we always pray to receive and maintain in the church of Christ?
7. What are the great advantages God's manifest presence can bring to us personally and in the church today?

SOME OF THE IMPORTANT THINGS WE CAN DO TO HELP US RECEIVE AND MAINTAIN GOD'S PRESENCE ALWAYS

Seeking and maintaining God's full presence and power all the time requires the fulfilment of several important conditions. But we want to be quick to add that seeking what to do to bring down God's presence and to maintain it all the time must not be limited to the church of Christ at large or to the local church. But we should remember that these same requirements are also necessary to help us to seek, to receive and to maintain God's personal revival. So we should go through this list of conditions and requirements with an open mind which incorporates concerns for both personal and corporate revivals. Some of these important requirements can be put together as follows:

1. We should always start this search with thorough spiritual and practical self-examination to remove all obstacles and impediments which can hinder and prevent our spiritual progress.
    Galatians 6:4
    But let each one examine his own work, and then he will have rejoicing in himself alone, and not in another. NKJV

    2 Corinthians 13:5
    Examine yourselves as to whether you are in the faith. Test yourselves. Do you not know yourselves, that Jesus Christ is in you? – unless indeed you are disqualified. NKJV

2. After such a self-examination, if we are found wanting in any areas of our spiritual and practical lives, we should be bold and sincere to start off with the prayer of confession and restitution
    1 John 1:9
    If we confess our sins, He is faithful and just to forgive us our sins and to cleanse us from all unrighteousness. NKJV

    Romans 10:10

For with the heart one believes unto righteousness, and with the mouth confession is made unto salvation. NKJV

3. We should be prayerful Christians whose prayer lives literally fulfils 1 Thessalonians 5:17.

<u>1 Thessalonians 5:17</u>

Pray without ceasing. NKJV

<u>Romans 8:15</u>

For you did not receive the spirit of bondage again to fear, but you received the Spirit of adoption by whom we cry out, "Abba, Father." NKJV

4. On this same matter of prayer, we should be Christians who understand that serious revival prayers sometimes call for long, medium or short periods of fasting.

<u>Matthew 9:14, 15</u>

Then the disciples of John came to Him, saying, "Why do we and the Pharisees fast often, but Your disciples do not fast?" And Jesus said to them, "Can the friends of the bridegroom mourn as long as the bridegroom is with them? But the days will come when the bridegroom will be taken away from them, and then they will fast. NKJV

<u>Joel 2:12</u>

"Now, therefore," says the Lord, "Turn to Me with all your heart, with fasting, with weeping, and with mourning." NKJV

5. Because seeking God's manifest presence can be hastened more by worship than most other activities, we should make the prayer of praise and worship an integral part of all revival prayers. **Worship is the highest form of prayer. It is the major prayer activity even in heaven.**

Ephesians 5:19-20

Speaking to one another in psalms and hymns and spiritual songs, singing and making melody in your heart to the Lord, giving thanks always for all things to God the Father in the name of our Lord Jesus Christ. NKJV

Psalm 42:1-2

As the deer pants for the water brooks, so pants my soul for You, O God. My soul thirsts for God, for the living /God. When shall I come and appear before God? NKJV

6. We should always cultivate the habit of reading and meditating upon God's word for constant spiritual upliftment.

Psalm 119:11

Your word I have hidden in my heart, that I might not sin against You. NKJV

Hebrews 4:12

For the word of God is living and powerful, and sharper than any two-edged sword, piercing even to the division of soul

and spirit, and of joints and marrow, and is a discerner of the thoughts and intents of the heart. NKJV

7. We should always be practical Christians who are careful to apply the word of God in our daily lives.
    <u>1 Corinthians 2:1-5</u>
    And I, brethren, when I came to you, did not come with excellence of speech or of wisdom declaring to you the testimony of God. For I determined not to know anything among you except Jesus Christ and Him crucified. I was with you in weakness, in fear, and in much trembling. And my speech and my preaching were not with persuasive words of human wisdom, but in demonstration of the Spirit and of power, that your faith should not be in the wisdom of men but in the power of God. NKJV

    <u>2 Timothy 3:16, 17</u>
    All Scripture is given by inspiration of God, and is profitable for doctrine, for reproof, for correction, for instruction in righteousness, that the man of God may be complete, thoroughly equipped for every good work. NKJV

8. We should fellowship and attend church services only in places where the unadulterated word of God is preached, where holiness and sanctification are upheld and practiced and the blessed Holy Spirit is allowed to operate freely.
    <u>1 Corinthians 3:16-17</u>

Do you not know that you are the temple of God and that the Spirit of God dwells in you? If anyone defiles the temple of God, God will destroy him. For the temple of God is holy, which temple you are. NKJV

<u>1 Corinthians 14:24-25</u>
But if all prophesy, and an unbeliever or an uninformed person comes in, he is convinced by all, he is convicted by all. And thus the secrets of his heart are revealed; and so, falling down on his face, he will worship God and report that God is truly among you. NKJV

9. We should always be heavenly-minded and heaven-focused to be able to avoid and overcome worldliness and worldly standards in our walk with God.
<u>Colossians 3:1</u>
If then you were raised with Christ, seek those things which are above, where Christ is, sitting at the right hand of God. NKJV

<u>Philippians 3:20</u>
For our citizenship is in heaven, from which we also eagerly wait for the Savior, the Lord Jesus Christ. NKJV

10. We must be people who know, understand and accept all the important biblical principles of practical holiness and sanctification in our daily lives.
<u>1 Peter 1:15, 16</u>

But as He who called you is holy, you also be holy in all your conduct, because it is written, "Be holy, for I am holy." NKJV

<u>Hebrews 12:14</u>
Pursue peace with all people, and holiness, without which no one will see the Lord. NKJV

11. We must be people who are free from all forms of sexual immorality and sexual deviations.
    <u>1 Corinthians 6:18-20</u>
    Flee sexual immorality. Every sin that a man does is outside the body, but he who commits sexual immorality sins against his own body. Or do you not know that your body is the temple of the Holy Spirit who is in you, whom you have from God, and you are not your own? For you were bought at a price; therefore glorify God in your body and in your spirit, which are God's. NKJV

    <u>1 Thessalonians 4:3</u>
    For this is the will of God, your sanctification: that you should abstain from sexual immorality. NKJV

12. We should cultivate the habit of sharing the good news of salvation with the unsaved people around us towards the fulfilment of the great commission.
    <u>Acts 1:8</u>

But you shall receive power when the Holy Spirit has come upon you; and you shall be witnesses to Me in Jerusalem, and in all Judea and Samaria, and to the end of the earth." NKJV

<u>Matthew 28:19, 20</u>
Go therefore and make disciples of all the nations, baptizing them in the name of the Father and of the Son and of the Holy Spirit, teaching them to observe all things that I have commanded you; and lo, I am with you always, even to the end of the age." Amen. NKJV

Anytime we learn what to do to be able to undertake an assignment successfully and in addition to this we learn the benefits which can accrue to us after the successful execution of this task, it gives us great encouragement and the necessary zeal to be able to undertake this assignment successfully. So after learning the importance of God's presence in our quest for revival and what to do in practical terms to be able to cultivate this divine presence, if in addition to this we are able to learn some of the benefits of this action, this knowledge will go a long way to help us to make all the necessary sacrifices to seek and maintain God's presence all the time. In consequence of this, we want to discuss some of the important benefits of receiving and maintaining God's presence as follows:

Bible Study and Personal Review Questions

1. How important is self-examination to our being able to pray in ways which can bring down God's presence?
2. What is the prayer of confession? What is its importance in the prayer for God's presence?
3. Generally, what is the importance of a life of consistent prayer to our being able to pray down God's presence regularly?
4. Is fasting necessary in our prayer for God's revival and God's presence? What are the reasons for your answer?
5. In what practical ways can the prayer of praise and worship be of great assistance in our revival prayers and prayers for God's presence?
6. How can the word of God also be of great assistance in our prayer for spiritual revival and renewal and for God's manifest presence?
7. In what important ways can we experience the full power in the written word of God through its practical application in our lives? How can this bring power to back our revival prayers and prayers for God's presence?
8. What contribution can Christian fellowship make towards our being able to pray to receive God's presence regularly.
9. In what ways can worldliness and worldly-mindedness hinder our prayers for God's presence?

What can be the solution to this unfortunate spiritual disposition?

10. What great help can our following practical holiness and sanctification offer us in our prayers for God's presence?

11. Can sexual immorality and the numerous forms of sexual deviation prevalent in the world and in most churches today help us to pray and secure God's presence?

12. What great contribution can our sharing the good news of salvation regularly with the unbelievers around us make towards our being able to receive God's personal and corporate presence?

SOME OF THE IMPORTANT BENEFITS OF RECEIVING AND MAINTAINING GOD'S PRESENCE
It is the presence of God which stabilizes and holds the whole of creation together. If God withdraws His presence from creation and concentrates only on His activities in heaven, the whole of creation both spiritually and physically will crumble together for lack of sustenance through the omnipresence and the omnipotent power of God. This alone is a very important universal benefit which will encourage us to seek God's presence in everything everywhere. Now let us ask ourselves this great question which relates to the Church and its ministries: What are some of the specific advantages we

can derive from maintaining God's permanent presence in the Church? There are several benefits including the following listed below:

I. **THIS WILL ALWAYS BRING US DIVINE ASSURANCE WITH DIVINE VICTORIES**

1. **It assures us of the constant provision of God's great omnipotent power**

Joshua 1:5

No man shall be able to stand before you all the days of your life; as I was with Moses, so I will be with you. I will not leave you nor forsake you. NKJV

Deuteronomy 20:4

For the Lord your God is He who goes with you, to fight for you against your enemies, to save you. NKJV

2. **It assures us of God's Companionship**

Psalm 16:11

You will show me the path of life; in Your presence is fullness of joy; at Your right hand are pleasures forevermore. NKJV

Hebrews 13:5

Let your conduct be without covetousness; be content with such things as you have. For He Himself has said, "I will never leave you nor forsake you." NKJV

3. **It assures us of God's help in Temptation**

<u>1 Corinthians 10:13</u>

No temptation has overtaken you except such as is common to man; but God is faithful, who will not allow you to be tempted beyond what you are able, but with the temptation will also make the way of escape, that you may be able to bear it. NKJV

4. **It assures us of God's comforting presence in our moments of discouragement.**

<u>Psalm 116:8-9</u>

For You have delivered my soul from death, my eyes from tears, and my feet from falling. I will walk before the Lord in the land of the living. NKJV

5. **It assures us of God's constant divine help and support**

<u>Psalm 46:1</u>

God is our refuge and strength, a very present help in trouble. NKJV

6. **It assures us of God's divine rest**

<u>Psalm 37:7</u>

Rest in the Lord, and wait patiently for Him; do not fret because of him who prospers in his way, because of the man who brings wicked schemes to pass. NKJV

<u>Matthew 11:28-30</u>

Come to Me, all you who labor and are heavy laden, and I will give you rest. Take My yoke upon you and learn

from Me, for I am gentle and lowly in heart, and you will find rest for your souls. For My yoke is easy and My burden is light." NKJV

Bible Study and Personal Review Questions
1. Who is the source of all the power we need in the church and in our personal lives? What assurance do we have that God's constant presence can always provide us with this power?
2. What assurance of divine companionship can we have in our maintaining God's divine presence? What advantages can this bring to us?
3. In what practical ways can God's presence help us in our moments of temptation? Without this help, what danger can temptations pose to our Christian lives?
4. When discouragements come to us as human beings, how does the abiding presence of God help to sustain us?
5. Who is our helper in the Christin race and on the Christian journey? What assurance do we have that God's presence will always provide us with this help?
6. What assurance of social and spiritual rest can the presence of God provide for us in the Church of Christ?

II. **THIS WILL ALWAYS BRING US SEVERAL SPIRITUAL BENEFITS**

1. **It is a great source of continuous spiritual Strength and Encouragement**
   Isaiah 40:31
   But those who wait on the Lord shall renew their strength; they shall mount up with wings like eagles, they shall run and not be weary, they shall walk and not faint. NKJV

   Psalm 105:4
   Seek the Lord and His strength; seek His face evermore! NKJV

2. **It is a great source of victory over the flesh**
   Galatians 5:16
   I say then: walk in the Spirit, and you shall not fulfil the lust of the flesh. NKJV

3. **It is a great source of faith and confidence**
   Romans 10:17
   So then faith comes by hearing, and hearing by the word of God. NKJV

   Psalm 23:4
   Yea, though I walk through the valley of the shadow of death, I will fear no evil; for You are with me; your rod and Your staff, they comfort me. NKJV

4. **It is a great source of spiritual fulfilment**
   Psalm 37:4
   Delight yourself also in the Lord, and He shall give you the desires of your heart. NKJV

Bible Study and Personal Review Questions
1. What is the sure way to get freedom from spiritual exhaustion as we continue to run the Christian race? How can our regularly being in the presence of God help provide us with the needed spiritual strength?
2. What danger can the flesh pose to our being able to finish the Christian race with success? How can the maintenance of God's presence always help us to conquer the flesh?
3. In what practical ways can God's presence constantly provide us with the faith and confidence we need in all the known phases of the Christian life?
4. What are some of the practical things in life which when put together and provided continually for us as Christians can be described as genuine fulfilment? What is the sure source of this fulfilment we need?

III. THIS WILL ALWAYS BRING US SEVERAL PRACTICAL BENEFITS
   1. **It is the source of increase of our Wisdom**
      Proverbs 2:1-6

My son, if you receive my words, and treasure my commands within you, so that you incline your ear to wisdom, and apply your heart to understanding; yes, if you cry out for discernment, and lift up your voice for understanding, if you seek her as silver, and search for her as for hidden treasures; then you will understand the fear of the Lord, and find the knowledge of God. For the Lord gives wisdom; from His mouth come knowledge and understanding. NKJV

2. **It is the source of increase of our Boldness**
    Acts 4:13
    Now when they saw the boldness of Peter and John, and perceived that they were uneducated and untrained men, they marveled. And they realized that they had been with Jesus. NKJV

3. **It is the source of increase of our Joy**
    Psalm 16:11
    You will show me the path of life; in Your presence is fullness of joy; at Your right hand are pleasures forevermore. NKJV

4. **It is the source of the increase of our Personal Peace**
    Isaiah 26:3

You will keep him in perfect peace, whose mind is stayed on You, because he trusts in You. NKJV

Bible Study and Personal Review Questions
1. What is wisdom? What is its importance to us as Christians? How can we receive it regularly?
2. What is boldness? What is its value to us as Christians today? How can we receive it regularly in the church today?
3. What is the importance of continuous joy to the successful Christian life? How can the presence of God provide us with this joy regularly?
4. In what practical ways can we say that both spiritual and social peace are necessary for our survival as Christians? How can the presence of God help provide us with this peace?

THE CHURCH HAS A DIVINE RESPONSIBILITY TOWARDS ITSELF

In a certain sense, the work of the church is comparable to the manufacturing process in the factory. Manufacturing always goes with the principle, "what you put in is what you get out." If you want to manufacture cloth, what you need to put into the machines is cotton. If you do that you will get the cloth. If you want to manufacture paper, you have to put pulp into the machines and your paper will eventually come out. Similarly, what the Church puts into its members is what it reaps practically in the life of the church. So it is always important for the church to sow good seeds in its members so that it can also reap the fruits of faithfulness, righteousness, purity, commitment and dedication from these same members.

In other words, if the church works hard to fulfill its internal responsibility towards its members and thereby toward itself, it gains both spiritual and practical advantages in the long run. This forms the subject of our discussion in this second section of the divine mandate given to the church. Let us start the details of the discussion this way:

SOME OF THE IMPORTATNT THINGS THE CHURCH CAN DO TO HELP BUILD UP THE BELIEVERS

The Church of the Lord Jesus Christ is not composed of angels but by ordinary sinful human beings who have been saved by the amazing grace of God and need help to grow and advance spiritually all the time. So as the church members make personal and individual efforts to be able to live aright for God and to maintain the burning fire of God in their spiritual lives, the church itself must also help them first with the provision of the appropriate atmosphere of continuous revival through regular renewal and spiritual restoration programmes to help them remain constantly sanctified and empowered for

God. This is regularly needed to enable the church to assist its members to grow and mature steadily so that later it can mobilize them to help it fulfil its responsibility towards itself and later towards the world.

Specifically, the church must also help all the members to benefit from the underlisted activities for them to continue to grow constantly and become useful to Christ. They are as follows:

1. To be able to experience the constant presence of God in their lives with all its numerous benefits.
2. To be taught personal evangelism and soul-winning to be able to make disciples as commanded in the Great Commission.
3. To be regular participants in the united services of the Church for full and regular spiritual edification.
4. To be taught to fully get involved in the united prayers of the church for their regular spiritual renewal, regular spiritual empowerment and regular spiritual advancement.
5. To be taught the importance of spiritual fellowship as provided by the church for their full and continuous participation.
6. To be taught the spiritual gifts of Christ and their operation in the church for general spiritual edification.

7. They should be taught spiritual faithfulness and accountability to God in their public, secret and family lives so as to induce practical holiness and practical sanctification from the lives of all committed church members.

8. They must be taught and encouraged to participate in all the sacraments and ordinances of the church.

It is important to reemphasize this great responsibility of the church towards its members because these members constitute its future army and workforce. So what the Church puts into them as suggested above and invests in them spiritually and practically is exactly what the church is going to reap in its ministry and progress.

But the church can fulfil these noble responsibilities towards its members only when it is alive spiritually through the regular spiritual revivals and renewals granted by the Holy Spirit. A dead church can only produce dead church members who are spiritually useless in the kingdom business of the church. But a vibrant and spiritually powerful church which is constantly renewed and energized by the Holy Spirit can always make useful investments in the lives of its members with all and even more of the spiritual virtues discussed above. Hence the need for regular mini and mega revivals in all the living churches of Christ.

Before we finish our discussion of this second mandate of the Church, let us give a little time to the discussion of practical holiness and sanctification because of their importance to the survival of the church in the contemporary society as well as the spiritual survival of the church itself in this end-time period.

Bible Study and Personal Review Questions
1. In what practical ways does the principle of sowing and reaping express itself in the ministry of the church?
2. Why would it be a sad mistake for a church to relax in its efforts to support its members to grow steadily, to be empowered regularly and to move towards spiritual maturity daily?
3. What are some of the spiritual activities which must be encouraged and made available in every local church to promote the general spiritual well-being of its members?
4. What are some of the practical programmes and activities the church should always take its members through to ensure their steady spiritual and practical growth and stability?
5. How can regular revivals and spiritual renewal programmes help every local church to execute this task faithfully?

6. What is the importance of holiness to the spiritual survival of individual believers and of the Church in general?

THE CHURCH MUST REGULARLY PREACH AND TEACH PRACTICAL HOLINESS AND SANCTIFICATION

One major area where the church keeps on failing and disappointing God is in the area of the fulfilment of its inward and internal responsibility towards itself especially as it relates to holiness and purity. Anytime and anywhere you see and hear people criticizing the church, it is the church's failure in this area. The church is supposed to be the light and the salt of the world. It is also to be a body of saved sinners who are sanctified and purified by Christ and the Holy Spirit. As a result of this, the church has been given a high spiritual and practical standard of holiness which can be fulfilled only in an atmosphere of continuous spiritual revivals, renewals and restoration.

But the church keeps failing in this area because we keep on ignoring the divine power and enablement of the Holy Spirit which are supplied in an atmosphere of revival and renewal to help us walk on this path of holiness and purity. The high standard of holiness for the Church can be read from passages like the following:

<u>1 Peter 1:15, 16</u>
But as He who called you is holy, you also be holy in all your conduct, because it is written, "Be holy, for I am holy." NKJV

<u>Matthew 5:48</u>
Therefore you shall be perfect, just as your Father in heaven is perfect. NKJV

<u>1 Thessalonians 4:3, 7</u>
For this is the will of God, your sanctification: that you should abstain from sexual immorality. For God did not call us to uncleanness, but in holiness. NKJV

<u>Philippians 2:14, 15</u>
Do everything without grumbling or arguing, so that you may become blameless and pure, "children of God without fault in a warped and crooked generation." Then you will shine among them like stars in the sky. NIV

This high practical standard of living has brought a great internal responsibility upon the church and all its members which must be fulfilled everywhere, every time and in all situations and circumstances. But ordinary human beings without the power of the Holy Spirit are weak creatures until the power of the Holy Spirit is poured upon us to help us to live in accordance with the Scriptures quoted above. And we can receive regular outpourings of this Holy Ghost power only through revivals and powerful spiritual renewal programmes. This is why we still need regular personal and corporate revivals in the church of the Lord Jesus Christ today.

Spiritual weakness leading to worldliness and lust can never produce sanctified lives! This is why it is often said that the Christian life practically is an impossible life without the full power of the Holy Spirit. It is not a life of boasting and mere rhetoric in saying all the time, "I will do it, I will do it." But it is a life fully energized and supported by the power of the Holy Spirit to do what is good, holy and righteous all the time without even talking about it. This is the only way we can live to fulfil the standards set in the references quoted above to fulfill the internal responsibility of holiness and sanctification within the church to the glory of God. A summary of the inward and internal responsibilities of the church can be presented to conclude this discussion as follows:

1. We need regular revivals to ensure spiritual continuity in the great work of the church.

2. Revival is necessary for us to maintain a sense of God's general presence and holiness in the church and a sense of our own personal holiness and sanctification for our spiritual progress.
3. Revival is necessary to bring continuous spiritual healing which results in continuous renewal to the church.
4. Revival is necessary for us to maintain God's full and beneficial manifest presence in the church.

Bible Study and Personal Review Questions
1. Why is the church always criticized by the world and unbelievers for its failures in practical sanctification and holiness?
2. What are some of the Bible references which talk about God's standards of holiness and purity of genuinely born-again believers?
3. Can these standards of spiritual and practical perfection be met without the constant fullness and support of the Holy Spirit?
4. In what ways do these standards of holiness and sanctification place an obligation upon the church to seek God's spiritual revivals and renewals regularly?
5. What summary can you give to the teachings in this section on the church's internal responsibility towards itself?

THE CHURCH HAS A DIVINE RESPONSIBILITY TOWARDS THE WORLD

The church has a divine responsibility towards the world. Though the church is not part of the world in the spiritual sense, the church exists to serve the world and its people with the propagation of the gospel and for the world also to serve the church by supplying it with regular converts. This is what we mean by saying that the church has a responsibility towards the world. The truth about missions and evangelism is that if the world can be evangelized, it is totally dependent upon the ministry of the church in worldwide missions and evangelism fully supported by the power of the Holy Spirit in an atmosphere of continuous revival and continuous spiritual renewal. This is what theologians describe as the church working towards the fulfilment of the Great Commission of the Lord Jesus Christ as it is stated in Matthew 28:18-20 in the words:

> *"Then Jesus came to them and said, "All authority in heaven and on earth has been given to me. Therefore go and make disciples of all nations, baptizing them in the name of the Father and of the Son and of the Holy Spirit, and teaching them to obey everything I have commanded you. And surely I am with you always, to the very end of the age."*
> NIV

Based upon this, let us sum up the church's responsibility towards the world as follows:

1. We need Revival if we are going to love the world and its salvation to the extent of being prepared to sacrifice for it.
2. We need Revival if we are going to answer the heart cry of the world in our generation for a saviour and for deliverance and freedom.
3. We need Revival if we are going to impact our communities and nations with sound Christian living and righteousness for Christ.

The sum total of whatever we have to say on the Church's third divine responsibility is that **we still need regular revivals in the worldwide church of Christ today to help us to work towards the fulfilment of the Great Commission given by Christ to take the gospel to all parts of the world as we have just read from Matthew 28:18-20.**

In other words, the church's existence on earth between now and the rapture which is variously described as the Church age, the period of grace and the dispensation of the Holy Spirit can also be aptly described as the "age of the Great Commission" during which period it is supposed to rely absolutely upon the Holy Spirit and the spiritual revivals He grants to impart divine power to be able to work to fulfil the Great Commission of sending the gospel and the message of salvation to all parts of the world. This great work of the church is what we want to discuss in this section together with its relation to God-given revivals. Let us start the discussion this way:

Bible Study and Personal Review Questions
1. Is it appropriate to say that the church has a divine responsibility towards the world and vice-versa?
2. What is this great responsibility the church has towards the world? What is the biblical basis for this claim?
3. When analysed carefully, what are some of the details of this divine mandate of the church towards the world?
4. What relationships have regular spiritual revivals and renewals in the church of Christ got with the fulfilment of its divine mandate in Matthew 28:18-20?

THE CHURCH OF THE LORD JESUS CHRIST NEEDS CONSTANT REVIVAL TO BE ABLE TO WORK TOWARDS THE FULFILMENT OF THE GREAT COMMISSION

It is an open truth as already emphasized that the Church of the Lord Jesus Christ can never work to fulfil the Great Commission given in Matthew 28:19-20 in an atmosphere of spiritual coldness, spiritual lethargy and spiritual decadence. The reason is that for this to take place successfully and continuously in the church, we need the constant and powerful presence of God to accompany His workers to be able to impart salvation through genuine conversion and where necessary, confirm the word with signs and wonders.

This underscores the truth that the great task of rescuing sinners from the dungeons and camps of the devil cannot be undertaken single-handedly in the church without the full presence and power of the Lord Jesus Christ and the blessed Holy Spirit in the atmosphere of revival we have been talking about. That was the reason why He gave the directive to the disciples and the would-be apostles to wait in Jerusalem to be filled with power from on high in a great and mighty outpouring before they start the work of worldwide evangelization. We read this from Luke 24:49 in the words: "Behold, I send the Promise of My Father upon you; but tarry in the city of Jerusalem until you are endued with power from on high."

Whatever we can do today to advance the gospel, we still need the full presence of Christ Himself and the full power of the Holy Spirit to be able to make impact and work to fulfil the Great Commission. If Christ inaugurated this task of worldwide evangelization with great power on the Day of Pentecost, can we continue this great work today and work successfully to be able to fulfil it before the rapture dawns in the power and energy of the flesh? Not at all!

This provides one of the major reasons why the true Church of the Lord Jesus Christ on earth today needs constant revival and spiritual renewal and awakening accompanied by the mighty power of the Holy Spirit to be able to get the needed strength, power and vigor to work to fulfil the Great Commission in this end-time period. What can we then do about this problem confronting the Church? The Word of God has the answer. Let us return to it for the following clear-cut answers and solutions:

Bible Study and Personal Review Questions
1. Is it true to say that the great task of evangelizing the world can be executed successfully only in an atmosphere of constant revival?
2. How can our cooperation with the Holy Spirit and with the Lord Jesus Christ Himself help us to work towards the fulfilment of the Great Commission with great success?
3. What great lessons do we get on this truth from Luke 24:49 and Acts 1:8?
4. What are some of the reasons which make all efforts made towards the fulfilment of the Great Commission in the energy of the flesh alone totally unprofitable?

Preliminary and General Observations

1. The Great Commission is a worldwide Commission which requires a very high spiritual standard to fulfil because it is not a local problem which requires only a local solution but a worldwide cross-border and cross-cultural assignment whose demands both materially and spiritually are immense.

   Mark 16:20

   And they went out and preached everywhere, the Lord working with them and confirming the word through the accompanying signs. Amen. NKJV

2. The Great Commission is a spiritual warfare. It is a warfare between us as missionaries and Satan and his demons as the attackers. They have imprisoned innocent people in the dungeons of sin and further blinded them to the light of the true gospel of liberation. Which soldier goes to war empty-handed without holding any defensive and offensive weapons? The Bible says the weapons of our warfare are spiritual and are released only when we pray and become spiritually active and fully revived for Christ.

   Ephesians 6:12

   For we do not wrestle against flesh and blood, but against principalities, against powers, against the rulers of the darkness of this age, against spiritual hosts of wickedness in the heavenly places. NKJV

<u>2 Corinthians 10:4</u>
For the weapons of our warfare are not carnal but mighty in God for pulling down strongholds. NKJV

3. If the Great Commission is a spiritual warfare, then it can only be fought successfully with continuous and intense personal and general intercessory prayer. This calls for our organizing "intercessory prayer armies" everywhere in the local church and generally in the church of Christ whose main work will be engaging in continuous intercessory prayer for missionaries, worldwide evangelization programmes as well as all local evangelistic events. If need be, such faithful intercessory armies must be supported with church funds to help its "prayer warriors" to give more of their time to this intercessory prayer programme. We need an atmosphere of continuous and intensive prayer and revival today to be able to work successfully to help fulfil the Great Commission before Christ returns.

4. The Great Commission is a call to discipleship and therefore requires carefully prepared and designed discipleship study materials which can help build up new converts spiritually until they reach the stage of spiritual maturity.

<u>Acts 2:42</u>

And they continued steadfastly in the apostles' doctrine and fellowship, in the breaking of bread, and in prayers. NKJV

5. Working towards the fulfilment of the Great Commission is not reserved for pastors, evangelists and other full-time workers of the church. Rather, the Great Commission calls for the recruitment and involvement of every true believer in every true local church of Christ worldwide in this task. This is a fact which requires universal revival and empowerment in the church of Christ and for that matter calls for the continuous personal revival of every true child of God in the church. So the fulfilment of the great commission can never occur in this end-time period unless the church organizes itself very well and prays for continuous personal and group revivals to bring down God's presence and power.

<u>Acts 8:4</u>

Therefore those who were scattered went everywhere preaching the word. NKJV

6. The history of all efforts towards the fulfilment of the Great Commission makes us aware that the work of evangelism and missions progress faster only in an atmosphere of intense prayer and continuous revivals.

7. The conclusion therefore is that regular and continuous revivals in the church are still needed everywhere to help us to become fully empowered all the time to work towards the fulfilment of the Great Commission. So what Christ promised before Pentecost in Luke 24:49 and caused it to happen at Pentecost in Acts 1:8 are still valid in the task of worldwide evangelization by the Church today.
Luke 24:49
Behold, I send the Promise of My Father upon you; but tarry in the city of Jerusalem until you are endued with power from on high." NKJV

Acts 1:8
But you shall receive power when the Holy Spirit has come upon you; and you shall be witnesses to Me in Jerusalem, and in all Judea and Samaria, and to the end of the earth."
NKJV

Bible Study and Personal Review Questions
1. What are the first three major characteristics of the Great Commission which make it mandatory for the

church and its members to be spiritually renewed and burning with the fire of the Holy Spirit before they make any efforts towards its fulfilment?

2. What is the importance of well-organized prayer armies and teaching towards the fulfilment of the Great Commission?

3. Are there some special people who are selected to work towards the fulfilment of the Great Commission or this work is the task of the worldwide body of Christ? What are the biblical proofs you have for your answer?

4. What personal and individual efforts can you henceforth start making in your own small way and in your own little corner towards the fulfilment of the Great Commission?

SOME PRACTICAL THINGS ALL THE REVIVED CHURCHES OF CHRIST CAN DO TOWARDS THE FULFILMENT OF THE GREAT COMMISSION

I. **We should pray for all the nations.**

<u>1 Timothy 2:1-2</u>

Therefore I exhort first of all that supplications, prayers, intercessions, and giving of thanks be made for all men, for kings and all who are in authority, that we may lead a quiet and peaceable life in all godliness and reverence. NKJV

II. **We should determine to talk about God's love to all the nations.**
Romans 5:8
But God demonstrates His own love toward us, in that while we were still sinners, Christ died for us. NKJV

John 3:16
For God so loved the world that He gave His only begotten Son, that whoever believes in Him should not perish but have everlasting life. NKJV

III. **We should pray to identify, carefully select and train brethren who have the call of God upon their lives to be able to engage in full-time worldwide evangelization.**
Acts 9:15
But the Lord said to him, "Go, for he is a chosen vessel of Mine to bear My name before Gentiles, kings, and the children of Israel. NKJV

2 Timothy 4:5
But you be watchful in all things, endure afflictions, do the work of an evangelist, fulfill your ministry. NKJV

Acts 2:39

For the promise is to you and to your children, and to all who are afar off, as many as the Lord our God will call." NKJV

IV. We should encourage and empower all committed local church members everywhere to get involved in missionary work and active soul-winning.

2 Timothy 2:15

Be diligent to present yourself approved to God, a worker who does not need to be ashamed, rightly dividing the word of truth. NKJV

Romans 10:14

How then shall they call on Him in whom they have not believed? And how shall they believe in Him of whom they have not heard? And how shall they hear without a preacher? NKJV

V. Above all, all genuinely born-again Christians in the Church of Christ who know and understand the value of the human soul must be encouraged to give freely to support evangelism and missions.

1 Corinthians 9:14

Even so the Lord has commanded that those who preach the gospel should live from the gospel. NKJV

2 Corinthians 9:6

But this I say: He who sows sparingly will also reap sparingly, and he who sows bountifully will also reap bountifully. NKJV

<u>Luke 6:38</u>
Give, and it will be given to you: good measure, pressed down, shaken together, and running over will be put into your bosom. For with the same measure that you use, it will be measured back to you." NKJV

<u>1 Timothy 6:17-19</u>
Command those who are rich in this present age not to be haughty, nor to trust in uncertain riches but in the living God, who gives us richly all things to enjoy. Let them do good, that they be rich in good works, ready to give, willing to share, storing up for themselves a good foundation for the time to come, that they may lay hold on eternal life. NKJV

Bible Study and Personal Review Questions
1. Why is the unity of all the revived churches of Christ necessary for the fulfilment of the Great Commission?
2. In this unity what can we do in the area of prayer to speed up the fulfilment of the Great Commission?
3. In this unity what can we do in the practical mobilization of workers to help in the fulfilment of the Great Commission?

4. In this unity, how can we regularly generate funds to finance evangelism and missions geared towards the fulfilment of the Great Commission?

REGULAR REVIVALS ARE STILL NEEDED IN THE CHURCH TO HELP IT AVOID THE PREDICTED END-TIME APOSTASY

The Bible has predicted terrible times of apostasy for the worldwide Church of Christ if the Church does not rise up to its spiritual responsibility of seeking God's constant spiritual revival, renewal and restoration. This great spiritual task of the church can only be fulfilled through intense prayer and other prayer activities organized with the intention of bringing down God's mighty power to bring total victory over sin, over the flesh and its works and to bring total victory over backsliding. We should always remember that though this great apostasy is predicted to occur in this end-time period just before the rapture occurs, it does not mean that the church should remain helpless, spiritually weak and completely incapacitated as these sad events take place.

God's purpose of giving us this warning in His foreknowledge was not to put fear into us and cause us to throw our hands up in despair and succumb to this spiritual devastation. Rather, He did this to forewarn us and help us to brace up and prepare against it with all the spiritual resources available to us in the church including regular and powerful revival and spiritual renewal programmes, power-packed prayer retreats, and constant mini and mega revival programmes. So we should all start making plans to be overcomers in this end-time period as we read the facts about this great apostasy in this end-time period just before the rapture. Let us look at the details of this biblical prediction as quoted from Pastor Stephen Adu-Boahen's book entitled: "The Rapture of the Church." It reads as follows:

The Sign of General Apostasy In the Church

Another specific sign which is also mentioned as going to occur before the rapture takes place for the events culminating in the end to begin is the general apostasy within the Christian Church. The Epistles have both predicted this apostasy and shown its nature and characteristics. Let us read about this from the scriptures:

> <u>2 Thessalonians 2:3</u>
> *"Let no one deceive you by any means; for that Day will not come unless the falling away comes first, and the man of sin is revealed, the son of perdition".*
> NKJV

Apostle Paul teaches in this passage that two great events are to take place before the Second Coming of Christ occurs. First, a falling away will occur. Because iniquity and lawlessness will increase, many will abandon their Christian faith, compromise it or remain nominal Christians. Secondly, the Antichrist, called the man of Sin will have to appear and work during the tribulation. It is only after this period, that Christ will come down in glory with His holy angels and saints. Paul goes further to show us the nature of this apostasy in two passages in 1 Timothy 4:1-3 and 2 Timothy 3:1-5. A close study of these two passages reveals that this end-time apostasy will take place in three major ways. First, there will be <u>intellectual apostasy.</u> Secondly, there will be <u>spiritual apostasy</u> and thirdly, there will be <u>moral apostasy.</u>

According to 1 Timothy 4:1, the **intellectual apostasy** will lead men to depart from the faith. They will either abandon the faith altogether or remain Christians by name. In the world today, the church has more of such apostate, nominal Christians than at any other time in the history of the Church. Another sign of intellectual apostasy according to 1 Timothy 4:2 is that church members will have their consciences seared with a hot iron. This tells us that their conscience will be hard and without feeling. They will therefore ignore the dictates of their conscience as Judas Iscariot did in the Gospels and freely get involved in sins and vices which are contrary to the Scriptures.

This intellectual apostasy will also show in the boldness with which men will teach false doctrines in the church. 1 Timothy 4:2 says such men will speak lies in hypocrisy, command men to abstain from marriage and certain foods, and help people to be more of unbelievers than believers. As a result, cardinal doctrines of evangelical Christianity such as the inspiration of the Scriptures, the belief in the miraculous and the supernatural, the deity of Christ and so on have all been ridiculed. Today people enter most theological institutes to be taught and made more unbelievers than believers. Is this intellectual apostasy not evident in your church?

Apart from this intellectual apostasy, **spiritual apostasy** was also predicted to characterize the end-time period. 1 Timothy 4:1 again says this spiritual apostasy will show in men giving heed to, and following deceiving demonic spirits and demon inspired doctrines. The upsurge of Satan-controlled prayer houses, and the proliferation of Satan inspired churches indulging in angel worship, mysticism and occultism in the world today is a clear evidence of this.

Another sign of this spiritual apostasy is what 2 Timothy 3:5 describes as men having a form of godliness but denying its power. Men will only be interested in possessing Christianity as a mere religion but will deny the true transforming power of the Holy Spirit which makes it a living religion by producing the new birth, breaking the power of sin in their lives and making them new creatures. Their Christianity will be on their lips but not in their hearts and lives.

Again, the two passages mention that there will also be a **Moral Apostasy**. 2 Timothy 3:1-4 makes a long list of the moral degradation that will occur among some Christians in the Church just before the end comes. It says men will be (1) self-lovers, (2) money lovers, (3) boastful and arrogant, (4) proud and haughty, (5) blasphemers who do not show any respect for God and for holy things, (6) self-willed, disobedient and undisciplined, (7) Unthankful for the blessings they receive from God and fellow men, (8) unholy, that is refusing to live to show any distinction between what is good, holy and pure and what is evil and sinful, (9) without natural affection - lack of love for their fellow men, (10) irreconcilable - that is unwilling to be appeased to be at peace with his fellows, (11) false accusers - slanderers who will falsely accuse their fellows like Satan, (12) incontinent - i.e. men who lack self-control, (13) fierce - savage and ferocious in their attitude, conduct and actions like animals, (14) despisers of those who are good and do good, (15) traitors - men who betray their fellows for personal gain, (16) headstrong -men who are self-willed and refuse to live under God's authority, (17) high-minded-men who are conceited and puffed up, (18) pleasure lovers rather than lovers of God.

Churches are today turning rapidly to be more of pleasure spots than power centres. Most churches give more time to parties, receptions, banquets, and sensuous love feasts than they give to genuine power-packed prayer meetings, Bible studies, and deliverance services. Where are we drifting today when we compare the present Church to that of the early church period in the Acts of the Apostles? If you do not know that the end of the world is near, and that the coming of the King is sooner than it has ever been, then look into your church and you will discover that the apostasy is ringing the bell of doom that you should get ready before you perish with the revelation of God's wrath against all the ungodliness of men.

Bible Study and Personal Review Questions
1. What spiritual picture has the word of God given about the Church in this end-time period in which we find ourselves?
2. What was God's main purpose of forewarning us about this state of the church many years ago? Is there anything the Church and its members can do about this prediction today to be able to avoid its devastations?

3. How is the predicted mass apostasy connected with the spiritual backslidings in the church today?

4. How can regular spiritual revivals and renewals help us to avoid this spiritual apostasy completely?

5. What is the first major area where this apostasy is predicted to show up? Are the practical signs predicted by the Bible not manifesting in this area in the church today? What evidence of this do you have in your own local Church?

6. What is the second major area where this predicted apostasy is supposed to show up? Is there any practical evidence that the things predicted to take place are occurring in this end-time period? How can they be avoided?

7. What is the third major area where the signs of this great apostasy are supposed to be manifested? Are they not truly occurring today? How can we escape their evil effects?

8. Putting all the spiritual ravages of this great end-time apostasy together, should we sleep and allow them to kill and destroy the spirituality and practical holiness of the church?

9. In what practical ways can we seek refuge in regular God-given spiritual revivals and renewals in the church of the Lord Jesus Christ today?

CHAPTER THREE

THE DIVINE SOURCE OF ALL TRUE REVIVALS IN THE CHURCH OF CHRIST

INTRODUCTION

In talking about the divine source of all the power behind all the revivals in the church of Christ, the one truth which must be brought out and understood is that there is no other divine source which can impart divine power to engender regular and continuous revivals in the Church apart from God the Father, God the Son and God the Holy Spirit! The underlying truth for this claim is that the church of Christ belongs to the Godhead in its entirety. If the church belongs to God in this way, then it logically and naturally follows that every useful activity in it including revivals can only occur with the full backing of the Spirit of God.

The Church is variously described in some biblical passages as the Church of God (1 Corinthians 10:32) "Give no offense, either to the Jews or to the Greeks or to the **church of God**"; the Church of Christ (Romans 16:16b)

"The **churches of Christ** greet you"; and the Church of the Holy Spirit (1 Corinthians 6:19) "Or do you not know that your body is the **temple of the Holy Spirit** who is in you, whom you have from God, and you are not your own?" So in talking about the divine source of power for all the revivals which can ever occur in the church of Christ, we want to be emphatic that the one and only true source of revival power in the church is the Holy Spirit of God.

In the passages quoted above, the Church is described as the "Church of God" and the "Churches of Christ." Individual believers who form the Church are described as the "temples of the Holy Spirit." So when they come together as a body of believers and as a local church, then the whole Church can be described as the temple of the Holy Spirit. If the church is God's church in this absolute sense, then let it be reemphasized that every activity in it can be done successfully only by the full operation of His Spirit. These important activities in the church include regular revivals which form the subject of this book.

How exactly does the Holy Spirit work in the Church to bring revival? This work is done conjunctly with the Father and the Lord Jesus Christ in an inseparable way. This means that the work of bringing regular revivals into the church of Christ has always been and will forever be the corporate work of the Godhead – the Father, the Son and the Holy Spirit. The Godhead has always been acting together in all major and important activities. They did this during the creation of man in Genesis 1:26.

> Genesis 1:26
> *Then God said, "**Let Us** make man in Our image, according to Our likeness; let them have dominion over the fish of the sea, over the birds of the air, and over the cattle, over all the earth and over every creeping thing that creeps on the earth." NKJV*

This unity of action also manifested at the baptism of Jesus. After the son had received the baptism physically, the heavens were opened and the Holy Spirit was seen visibly in the form of a dove descending upon Him. At the same time, God's word thundered from heaven saying "This is My beloved Son, in whom I am well pleased."

> Matthew 3:16, 17
> *When He had been baptized, Jesus came up immediately from the water; and behold, the heavens were opened to Him, and He saw the Spirit of God descending like a dove and alighting upon Him. And suddenly a voice came from heaven, saying, "This is My beloved Son, in whom I am well pleased." NKJV*

This same divine tri-unity of action occurs whenever and wherever God's genuine revival breaks out in the church of Christ. So it will be inaccurate to call any revival the revival of the Holy Spirit alone without mentioning God and Christ. In the same way, it would be most inappropriate to describe any revival as a revival of Christ without mentioning God and the Holy Spirit just as it would also be incomplete to describe any revival as God's revival without bringing the Lord Jesus Christ and the Holy Spirit into the picture. With this in view, we are going to discuss the divine source of all true revivals in this chapter by mentioning the whole Godhead – Father, Son and the Holy Spirit.

THE LORD GOD AS OUR SOURCE OF SPIRITUAL REVIVAL AND RENEWAL

BIBLICAL TEACHING ON THE LORD GOD AS THE GREAT SOURCE OF THE SPIRITUAL REVIVAL AND RENEWAL OF HIS PEOPLE

<u>Isaiah 57:15</u>
For this is what the high and exalted One says – he who lives forever, whose name is holy: "I live in a high and holy place, but also with the one who is contrite and lowly in spirit, to revive the spirit of the lowly and to revive the heart of the contrite. NIV

<u>Psalm 80:18</u>
Then we will not turn away from you; revive us, and we will call on your name. NKJV

<u>Psalm 119:25</u>
I am laid low in the dust; preserve my life according to your word. NIV

In the few biblical passages quoted above, the truth is strongly brought out that God is the great source of the revival of His people. We read from the passage quoted from the prophet Isaiah that when the conditions for revival are provided, then God becomes the God who "revives the spirit of the lowly and revives the heart of the contrite." In consequence of this, prayer for revival and spiritual renewal is directed to Him in Psalm 80:18 in the words, "revive us, and we will call on your name." It is for this same reason that the Psalmist in Psalm 119:25 also cries to God for revival, renewal and spiritual restoration in the words, "preserve my life according to your word." Whenever God brings us revival in the ways discussed above, this always results in perfect spiritual renewal for us as indicated in the references quoted below:

<u>Ephesians 4:23</u>
To be made new in the attitude of your minds.
NIV

<u>Romans 12:2</u>
*Do not conform to the pattern of this world, but be transformed **by the renewing of your mind**. Then you will be able to test and approve what God's will is — his good, pleasing and perfect will.* NIV

<u>2 Corinthians 4:16</u>
*Therefore we do not lose heart. Though outwardly we are wasting away, yet **inwardly we are being renewed day by day**.* NIV

<u>Colossians 3:10</u>
*And have put on the new self, **which is being renewed in knowledge in the image of its Creator**.* NIV

<u>Titus 3:5</u>
He saved us, not because of righteous things we had done, but because of his mercy. He saved us through

Knowing that God is the great source of our spiritual revival and renewal as we have learnt above is not enough. We need to go further to find out what to do to be able to receive this revival regularly and continually. In addition, we need to raise our expectation to know and be certain of some of the changes we want to see in our spiritual and practical lives as this revival and renewal occur. Furthermore, we must be sure and certain of some of the important blessings of renewal this can bring to us so that we will not miss any of these great blessings when the grace, mercy and power of God cause them to start coming into our lives. These are what we have put together in this sub-section as the important truths to know about God's spiritual revivals and renewals some of which can be listed below as follows:

Bible Study and Personal Review Questions
1. What proofs do we have from Isaiah 57:15, Psalm 80:18 and Psalm 119:25 that the Lord God is our great source of spiritual revival and spiritual renewal?
2. Whenever God grants us spiritual revival and spiritual renewal, which one major area does this affect according to the following references? (Ephesians 4:23; Romans 12:2; 2 Corinthians 4:16)

3. Whenever God's spiritual renewal begins in the mind as we have discovered in the previous section, how does this affect our entire system according to Colossians 3:10?

4. By what means does God effect His spiritual renewal and spiritual revival in our lives according to Titus 3:5?

SOME IMPORTANT TRUTHS TO NOTE ABOUT GOD'S SPIRITUAL REVIVALS AND SPIRITUAL RENEWALS

1. Whenever we receive God's spiritual revivals, we obtain complete spiritual renewal.

The dictionary meaning of renewal is the work of returning something to its original state of perfection and newness after undergoing an unfortunate process of distortion, destruction and unacceptable change. This truth is brought out this way. The word "re" which means again whenever it is added to the word "new" means making something new again as it was originally. Renewal therefore presupposes that somewhere along the way, that which was perfect and good became no more and necessitated a return of firm action to seek its replacement or restoration.

Seeking the spiritual renewal and the spiritual revival God grants to His people must also conform to this explanation. After our salvation, we were in a good and perfect spiritual state initially until some of the normal sins usually called "revival killers" came into our lives with time to initiate an unfortunate downward process of spiritual declension. When we receive the spiritual revival and renewal God grants, we do not continue to remain in this state of total spiritual backwardness anymore but we are brought back to our initial state of newness to become brand new persons spiritually.

2. **God's spiritual revivals and renewals come to us only when we realize our spiritual helplessness and hopelessness and cry to Him for spiritual restoration.** We receive God's spiritual revivals and renewals only when we sense and give a clear spiritual indication and signal that we need them. When we realize our spiritual hopelessness and the imminent spiritual destructions which can accompany this and take the bold step of crying to God for His mercy, spiritual support, spiritual renewal and spiritual restoration, He always hears our cry. When King David came into this unfortunate spiritual state and saw his need for God's immediate spiritual revival, renewal and restoration, he cried to God in the words of Psalm 51:1, 2 which says "Have mercy upon me, O God, according to Your lovingkindness; according to the multitude of Your tender mercies, blot out my transgressions. Wash me

thoroughly from my iniquity, and cleanse me from my sin." And God heard his prayer immediately.

3. **Spiritual Renewals are granted by God only when we become specific in confessing our sins, shortcomings and acts of backsliding for his mercy, forgiveness and complete restoration.**

   We need to be open about our sins and boldly confess them to God for total forgiveness before we can receive any spiritual revivals and renewals from the Holy God. When the prodigal son returned to the father, what example of this does he give to us in the Scriptures? He was specific in telling his father in Luke 15:21 that "Father, I have sinned against heaven and in your sight, and am no longer worthy to be called your son." This is the example of direct and open confession God requires for our immediate spiritual restoration.

   If the sins committed involve acts of sexual immorality and sexual deviation like fornication, adultery and the like, they must not be generalized but specifically confessed for total cleansing and forgiveness. Whenever you hide your sins, God does not take you serious enough to forgive, cleanse and restore you spiritually because in His omnipresence, he was at that place where you committed these sins before you got there. So trying to hide them from Him smacks of unfaithfulness and insincerity of repentance. (1 John 1:9)

4. **To receive God's spiritual renewals, we need to determine with the help and power of the Holy Spirit to break free from all forms of spiritual and practical compromise.**

   The sin of compromise is a major revival killer because it works insidiously, slowly and imperceptibly but it is very destructive spiritually. It caused the spiritual downfall of King Solomon when he started marrying heathen wives contrary to the clear instructions of God to all the Kings of Israel (Deuteronomy 17:17). It was also responsible for the many backslidings of Israel during the time of the judges.

   Today, it is operating as a major revival killer in the Church with the involvement of many believers in acts like spiritual idolatry, involvement in spiritism and occultism, involvement in Satan-controlled social groups and secret societies, pride, new world reasoning, falsehood and social pretence, unwholesome speech, illicit sexual relationships, unequal yoking of believers and unbelievers in marriage, broken homes over unbiblical trivialities, open tolerance of both grave and so-called little sins and relaxation of clear biblical principles in daily practical actions. (Proverbs 1:10)

5. **To receive God's spiritual renewal, we need to rely upon Christ and the power of the Holy Spirit to break free from all the common forms of worldliness.**

    Worldliness which is copying the behaviour and customs of the unregenerate world of unbelievers around us is also a major revival killer we need to repent of before we can receive God's spiritual revivals and renewals at any time. We are told to shun this world in James 4:4 and 1 John 2:15-17. Today, worldliness also shows in things like indiscipline and lack of restraint that leads to ungodly pursuits out of self-interest, lust after ecclesiastical positions and power and several other forms of unfaithfulness which go contrary to God's word in preference for popular but sinful worldly values and standards.

    Worldliness further shows in wilful neglect of God's work, ecclesiastical in-fightings leading to constant discord and self-serving agendas. It is also responsible for the disloyal leadership in most churches today. But we can never be for Christ and at the same time be for the world. This is the clear message of James 4:4. So if we truly want God's revival and renewal, then we must also be prepared to shun all forms of worldliness.

    James 4:4

Adulterers and adulteresses! Do you not know that friendship with the world is enmity with God? Whoever therefore wants to be a friend of the world makes himself an enemy of God. NKJV

1 John 2:15-17

Do not love the world or the things in the world. If anyone loves the world, the love of the Father is not in him. For all that is in the world — the lust of the flesh, the lust of the eyes, and the pride of life — is not of the Father but is of the world. And the world is passing away, and the lust of it; but he who does the will of God abides forever. NKJV

6. **To obtain God's spiritual renewal, we need to confess and change from the neglect of our spiritual disciplines.**

In the same way that a new and well-manufactured car can never move unless it runs on some form of energy as an electric car or a car which runs on some form of fossil fuel like petrol and diesel, so can't we also get the needed spiritual strength and spiritual power to be able to work for God successfully if we neglect our spiritual disciplines which lead us to study the word of God regularly, to give ourselves to prayer sometimes with fasting and to seek God's spiritual renewals regularly.

The lack or the relaxation of our spiritual disciplines can lead to spiritual coldness resulting in many unfortunate incidents in the ministry. This can lead to careless handling of the word, powerlessness in ministry, and carnality in handling church matters and church affairs. So if we truly need God's spiritual revivals and renewals, we must go back and pick up our spiritual disciplines so that after our repentance and restoration we will not relapse into this state of spiritual coldness and degeneration. (1 Peter 2:2; Isaiah 40:31; 1 Thessalonians 5:17)

CONCLUDING NOTE

If we truly desire God's continuous spiritual revivals and renewals, He is ever prepared to impart them to us whenever we get ready to do away with the "revival and renewal killers" discussed above. God knows that He is the only true source of our spiritual revivals and renewals so whenever we make any sincere effort to seek His revival, He meets us half-way with important Bible passages like the ones listed below to bring us perfect spiritual and practical restoration. They are as follows:

<u>Isaiah 1:18, 19</u>

"Come now, and let us reason together," says the Lord, "Though your sins are like scarlet, they shall be as white as snow; though they are red like

crimson, they shall be as wool. If you are willing and obedient, you shall eat the good of the land. NKJV

Isaiah 44:22

I have blotted out, like a thick cloud, your transgressions, and like a cloud, your sins. Return to Me, for I have redeemed you." NKJV

Micah 7:18-19

Who is a God like You, pardoning iniquity and passing over the transgression of the remnant of His heritage? He does not retain His anger forever, because He delights in mercy. He will again have compassion on us, and will subdue our iniquities. You will cast all our sins into the depths of the sea. NKJV

Isaiah 3:10

"Say to the righteous that it shall be well with them, for they shall eat the fruit of their doings. NKJV

Bible Study and Personal Review Questions
1. What are the practical details involved in the spiritual revivals and renewals granted by God? In specific terms, what happens to us when we genuinely become revived and renewed?

2. According to Psalm 51:1, 2 what is the first spiritual attitude to adopt if we sincerely want to receive God's spiritual renewal?

3. What is the second important spiritual attitude to adopt in God's presence if we are truly eager to seek and obtain His spiritual renewal? What clues do the following references provide to help us? (Luke 15:21; 1 John 1:9)

4. What is the sin of compromise? In what practical way does it manifest in the Church today?

5. What danger can compromise pose to our search for God's spiritual renewal? What is the best way to deal with this sin of compromise to open the door for God's spiritual renewal to come to us? (Deuteronomy 17:17; Proverbs 1:10)

6. What is worldliness, how can it also be a great impediment in our search for God's true spiritual renewal (James 4:4)? How does worldliness show in our personal lives and in the life of the church today? How can we conquer worldliness? (1 John 2:15-17)

7. What do we call in the Church "the Christian's spiritual disciplines?" according to the following references? (1 Peter 2:2; Isaiah 40:31; 1 Thessalonians 5:17)

8. What great assurances do we have from the Scriptures that no matter what happens if we sincerely desire

God's spiritual renewal we can receive it? (Isaiah 1:18, 19; Isaiah 44:22; Micah 7:18-19; Isaiah 3:10)

THE LORD JESUS CHRIST AS OUR SOURCE OF SPIRITUAL REVIVAL AND RENEWAL

As already explained at the beginning of this chapter, in talking about the divine source of all the revivals in the church, we can never dispense with the Lord God, the Lord Jesus Christ and the Holy Spirit. After discussing the Lord God as the great source of revival in part one of this chapter, we want to look at the Lord Jesus Christ as another great source of all the revivals in the Church in part 2 of this chapter. We will further explore in this second section that knowing the Lord Jesus Christ as the source of your revival can never be complete without our going further to seek how and where Christ grants us this revival in our personal lives and in the life of the church at large. Let us now proceed to examine some facts on this beginning with the following biblical passages.

SOME BIBLICAL PASSAGES ON CHRIST AS THE SOURCE OF OUR REVIVAL AND SPIRITUAL RENEWAL

Romans 12:2

*And do not be conformed to this world, but be transformed **by the renewing of your mind**, that you may prove what is that good and acceptable and perfect will of God.* NKJV

2 Corinthians 5:17
*Therefore, if anyone is in Christ, **he is a new creation**; old things have passed away; behold, **all things have become new**.* NKJV

2 Corinthians 5:19
*That is, that God was in Christ reconciling the world to Himself, **not imputing their trespasses to them**, and has committed to us the word of reconciliation.* NKJV

Ephesians 2:10
*For we are His workmanship, **created in Christ Jesus for good works**, which God prepared beforehand that we should walk in them.* NKJV

John 3:5
*Jesus answered, "Most assuredly, I say to you, **unless one is born of water and the Spirit**, he cannot enter the kingdom of God.*

Romans 8:1
*There is therefore now no condemnation to those who are in Christ Jesus, **who do not walk according to the flesh**, but according to the Spirit.* NKJV

<u>Romans 8:9, 10</u>

But you are not in the flesh but in the Spirit, if indeed the Spirit of God dwells in you. Now if anyone does not have the Spirit of Christ, he is not His. **And if Christ is in you, the body is dead because of sin, but the Spirit is life because of righteousness.** NKJV

<u>Philippians 3:20-21</u>

For our citizenship is in heaven, from which we also eagerly wait for the Savior, the Lord Jesus Christ, **who will transform our lowly body that it may be conformed to His glorious body,** *according to the working by which He is able even to subdue all things to Himself.* NKJV

Bible Study and Personal Review Questions
1. Which of these biblical references do mention or at least allude to the fact that Jesus is a great source of our spiritual revivals and renewals?
2. Which of these references do mention that anytime we receive the spiritual renewals of Christ these translate into some practical changes in our lives?
3. Just like the Lord God, what spiritual collaboration goes on between Christ and the Holy Spirit in the process of our spiritual revival and renewal?

CHRIST AND OUR SPIRITUAL REVIVALS AND RENEWALS

We all know and understand fully well that the Lord Jesus Christ is another great source of our spiritual revival, spiritual renewal and spiritual restoration. All the Bible passages listed above do emphasize in some portions that just as we learnt about the Lord God that He is the great source of our spiritual revivals and renewals, the Lord Jesus Christ also does these same spiritual good works in all those who truly repent, accept and receive Him as their saviour. These truths are highlighted in the appropriate portions of the Scriptures. But how exactly does He work to do this for us in practical terms? Knowing this truth is very important because it can help us to prepare very well to meet Christ halfway to speed up the process of our spiritual revival and renewal.

Let me start by mentioning that seeking and receiving Christ's continuous revivals must be approached from three major angles. First, it should begin by our being fully in Him as saved persons. Secondly, this renewal can be firmly established only by our bearing practical proofs of salvation and new birth. And thirdly, this revival and the accompanying renewal can be granted only when we are prepared to do what can help us to sustain it all the time until Christ comes to take us home.

1. **Salvation and the Revivals granted by Christ**
   Starting with the first condition, it is clear from the Holy Scriptures that salvation begins every process of

revival in the life of the individual seeker. "But as many as received Him, to them He gave the right to become children of God, to those who believe in His name." (John 1:12). To qualify to receive Christ's revival and renewal regularly, you must fully belong to Him. That is, you must first repent to become a true child of God. You must also be sure that you truly belong to Him. This is the essence of "As many as received Him."

2. **Practical Proofs of Salvation and the Revivals granted by Christ**

   The second main thing to do to qualify to receive Christ's constant revivals and renewals is our bearing the practical fruits of repentance and salvation to back our claim of being truly born again and belonging to the Lord Jesus Christ. This can be read from several Bible passages including 2 Corinthians 5:17, "Therefore, if anyone is in Christ, he is a new creation; old things have passed away; behold, all things have become new." False, deceptive and spurious conversions can never bring us any continuous spiritual revivals and renewals from Christ.

   If your conversion is not genuine for you to become a new creature in the practical sense, then you do not need any revival from God because you are still dead in sins and trespasses. It means you have never been quickened spiritually. So if spiritually you are still dead in your sins and trespasses, why do you bother to come to Christ for revival? You have never been made new to be renewed! Several other Bible passages talk about our *"becoming new creatures"* after our genuinely repenting and giving ourselves to Christ. (Ezekiel 11:19, 20; John 3:3)

3. **Firmness and Commitment and the Revivals granted by Christ**

The third important truth to note on this question of seeking and receiving continuous spiritual revivals and renewals from Christ is the problem of spiritual firmness and commitment after our salvation. Though we can be genuinely saved but because we are still living in this sinful world with unbelievers, we are still living with the presence of sin. So at times we can meet several spiritual and practical challenges which will demand that we renew ourselves spiritually all the time to be able to persevere in the Christian race as we at the same time undertake the Christian journey.

This is where the question of firmness and commitment which are required to bring Christ's constant spiritual revivals and spiritual renewals come in. This is echoed in Romans 12:2 which reads, *"And do not be conformed to this world, but be transformed by the renewing of your mind, that you may prove what is that good and acceptable and perfect will of God."* NKJV. This passage is calling upon us to seek spiritual renewals constantly so that we can keep on receiving the fresh energy, power and the strength of the Holy Spirit in what is called in this book "spiritual revivals and spiritual renewals".

This renewal comes to us from two sources. The first source is personal and the second source is divine. The first one demands that we make personal efforts through prayer, Bible study and other important spiritual disciplines to initiate the spiritual renewal. The second one demands that we complement our personal efforts with total dependence upon Christ to help us attain these constant spiritual renewals. This puts emphasis on the Lord Jesus Christ being our second major source of spiritual revivals and renewals. But we can obtain this renewal regularly only when we are also prepared to do our little part to pave the way for God's grace to be poured upon us in this regard.

Bible Study and Personal Review Questions
1. What is the importance of salvation to our receiving the spiritual revivals and spiritual renewals granted by the Lord Jesus Christ? (John 1:12)

2. What is the importance of the practical evidence of New Birth to our being able to receive the regular spiritual revivals and spiritual renewals of Christ?

3. Why is it both illogical and impossible for those who have not been genuinely born again with the practical evidence of new birth to pray for the revivals and renewals granted by Christ?

4. What are spiritual firmness and spiritual commitment? After our salvation, how do they come into this great question of receiving the regular spiritual revivals and renewals of Christ?

5. What are the two major things to do to be able to receive Christs' spiritual renewals and revivals anytime they are needed?

SOME PRACTICAL DIMENSIONS TO OUR SEEKING AND RECEIVING THE SPIRITUAL RENEWALS AVAILABLE IN CHRIST

As already explained above, seeking the spiritual renewal available in and through Christ requires the combination of our personal efforts and the grace of God imparted through Christ to assist us. In the light of this, we want to mention a few personal attitudes to adopt to help speed up this search for personal spiritual renewal anytime we say that we need and desire it.

1. We must renew our salvation and New Birth constantly to make sure that we are still holding them

and are still on track and are running the Christian race with all the seriousness it demands. This will inevitably lead us to ascertain whether we are still set on the Christian journey with the great determination to finish it with Christ.

<u>Titus 3:3-5</u>

For we ourselves were also once foolish, disobedient, deceived, serving various lusts and pleasures, living in malice and envy, hateful and hating one another. But when the kindness and the love of God our Savior toward man appeared, not by works of righteousness which we have done, but according to His mercy He saved us, through the washing of regeneration and renewing of the Holy Spirit. NKJV

2. We must check, review and renew our spiritual lives to ensure that the old life is still totally discarded and that we are still holding on firmly to the new life we received from Christ after our salvation. This is one area which the "revival killers" always target to be able to draw us back into backsliding.

<u>Ephesians 4:22-24</u>

That you put off, concerning your former conduct, the old man which grows corrupt according to the deceitful lusts, and be renewed in the spirit of your mind, and that you put on the new man which was created according to God, in true righteousness and holiness. NKJV

3. We also need to seek constant renewal in the knowledge of God and Christ. The mind matters in Christian experience because you are able to practise and follow only that which you fully know and understand. Consequently, if we want to maintain our spiritual renewal all the time, then we must make every effort to grow and increase in the knowledge of God through persistent and consistent study of God's word.

<u>Colossians 3:10</u>

And have put on the new man who is renewed in knowledge according to the image of Him who created him. NKJV

4. We must also be careful never to relapse into worldliness and worldly living. James 4:4 tells us that forever and ever anytime we get the desire to compromise with and become friends of the world, this can spiritually be interpreted as becoming the enemies of God. Though we are all living in the physical world together with all unbelievers, spiritually, Christians are not of the world which means they are not part of the world. Our focus, values and standards are always different from those of the world of unbelievers. So anytime we become one with the world and the same as the world, it means we have backslidden as Christians.

<u>James 4:4</u>

Adulterers and adulteresses! Do you not know that friendship with the world is enmity with God? Whoever therefore wants to be a friend of the world makes himself an enemy of God. NKJV

<u>Romans 12:2</u>
And do not be conformed to this world, but be transformed by the renewing of your mind, that you may prove what is that good and acceptable and perfect will of God. NKJV

Bible Study and Personal Review Questions
1. What is the importance of maintaining our spiritual walk and enlistment in the Christian race to our being able to receive the regular spiritual revivals and renewals of Christ? (Titus 3:3-5)
2. What is the importance of always making a difference between our old life in sin and our new life in Christ to our being able to access the spiritual revivals and renewals of Christ regularly? (Ephesians 4:22-24)
3. What is the importance of our increasing regularly in the knowledge of God and Christ to our being able to seek and receive the regular spiritual renewals of Christ? (Colossians 3:10)
4. How can our continually making a difference between us and the world contribute to our receiving the constant spiritual revivals and spiritual renewals of Christ? (James 4:4; Romans 12:2)

THE HOLY SPIRIT AS OUR SOURCE OF SPIRITUAL REVIVAL AND RENEWAL

Just like the Lord Jesus Christ, the Holy Spirit can never grant us any spiritual revivals, renewals and restorations until He is absolutely sure that we belong to Him totally through the salvation available to us in Christ. What is our basis for making this claim? Our biblical basis is found in the Scripture which reads, "Most assuredly, I say to you, unless one is born again, he cannot see the kingdom of God. Jesus answered, "Most assuredly, I say to you, unless one is born of water and the Spirit, he cannot enter the kingdom of God." (John 3:3, 5).

Revival is for those who are saved, truly born again and are fully admitted into God's holy kingdom of the righteous. It is not for unbelievers. Revival meetings can be organized to help bring unbelievers and sinners to repentance to be able to receive God's free salvation. But after such evangelistic revivals, those who will qualify to receive the continuous spiritual revivals and renewals of the Holy Spirit are those who after receiving Christ initially at these meetings will further decide to walk with Him and continue to stay in the church to be able to work out their salvation with fear and trembling.

It is worthy to note right from the beginning that the revivals granted by the Holy Spirit are often accompanied by great outward signs and manifestations of great power which often attract public attention and sometimes even work to also benefit these outsiders. Practical examples of the revivals and renewals granted by the Holy Spirit can be seen in what happened on the Day of Pentecost, in the vision of the dry bones and in the outpouring of the Holy Spirit in the house of Cornelius.

The church needed a great spiritual revival at Pentecost to commence the programme of worldwide evangelization and also to be able to penetrate the dark world of sin to bring the salvation of Christ to mankind. A great and unsurpassed spiritual revival was necessary to bring this about. By what means did God grant this revival? On the Day of Pentecost, it came down in Jerusalem as the revival of the Holy Spirit. The whole process began with the Holy Spirit moving as a rushing mighty wind, entering the upper room, filling all the disciples and settling on them like tongues of fire. This began the programme of the worldwide evangelization by the church beginning with the people of different nationalities who had gathered in Jerusalem to celebrate the Passover feast! We see this special activity of the Holy Spirit in the passage quoted as follows:

Acts 2:1-4

When the Day of Pentecost had fully come, they were all with one accord in one place. And suddenly there came a sound from heaven, as of a rushing mighty wind, and it filled the whole house where they were sitting. Then there appeared to them divided tongues, as of fire, and one sat upon each of them. And they were all filled with the Holy Spirit and began to speak with other tongues, as the Spirit gave them utterance. NKJV

Today, the Holy Spirit is continuing to grant this same level of revival to those who desire it and fill them so that they can continue in this worldwide evangelization programme to help fulfil the great commission. The Holy Spirit has another great lesson for us on His infillings with what happened in the house of Cornelius which can be read from the Book of Acts as follows:

<u>Acts 10:44-46a</u>
While Peter was still speaking these words, the Holy Spirit fell upon all those who heard the word. And those of the circumcision who believed were astonished, as many as came with Peter, because the gift of the Holy Spirit had been poured out on the Gentiles also. For they heard them speak with tongues and magnify God. NKJV

The great lessons we can learn here about the revivals granted by the Holy Spirit is that such revivals can also come to us as personal and family level revivals. It is true that revivals can come to us at the general church level. But we can experience these same Holy Ghost revivals in smaller fellowships.

In the vision of the dry bones (Ezekiel 37:1-10), what actually brought the revival to the bones which are symbols and examples of our being able to receive the revivals granted by the Holy Spirit today if we fulfil the conditions required for this is that, the revival came by the Spirit of God working miraculously on the bones to put them together and bring flesh upon them to cause the impossible to become possible.

The conclusion and great warning on this whole issue of revivals granted by the Holy Spirit in question form is this. With the predicted backslidings, compromise with sin, worldliness and mass falling away through the deceptive tactics of Satan and the antichrist in this end-time period, are we going to continue to stay in spiritual lukewarmness to miss Christ, His salvation and constant spiritual revivals and renewals? The inevitable answer should be: "In the mighty name of the Lord Jesus, this should never happen." To help us avoid this totally and permanently, let us read and meditate upon the following biblical passages which assure us that the Holy Spirit is our third great source of spiritual revivals and renewals just like the Lord God and the Lord Jesus and that we must rely upon Him for this grace all the time.

SOME BIBLICAL PASSAGES ON THE HOLY SPIRIT AS THE THIRD GREAT SOURCE OF OUR SPIRITUAL REVIVAL AND RENEWAL

Titus 3:5

*Not by works of righteousness which we have done, but according to His mercy He saved us, through the washing of regeneration **and renewing of the Holy Spirit.*** NKJV

Romans 8:11

*But if the Spirit of Him who raised Jesus from the dead **dwells in you**, He who raised Christ from the dead **will also give life to your mortal bodies through His Spirit who dwells in you.*** NKJV

Romans 8:26

*Likewise **the Spirit also helps in our weaknesses**. For we do not know what we should pray for as we ought, but **the Spirit Himself makes intercession for us with groanings which cannot be uttered.*** NKJV

Ephesians 1:13

In Him you also trusted, after you heard the word of truth, the gospel of your salvation; **in whom also, having believed, you were sealed with the Holy Spirit of promise.** *NKJV*

Bible Study and Personal Review Questions
1. Who is the third great source of the spiritual revivals and renewals we need as Christians?
2. Who are those who qualify to receive the regular spiritual revivals and renewals of the Holy Spirit? What scriptural proofs do we have on this?
3. How did the events which occurred on the Day of Pentecost take place? What special lessons do we learn from this great event on those who qualify to receive the revivals and empowerments of the Holy Spirit?
4. What great lessons can we gather about those who qualify to receive the renewals and infillings of the Holy Spirit in what occurred in the house of Cornelius?
5. Even though the revival granted in the vision of the dry bones came by the united action of the Godhead who was God's chief agent in the whole process. What lessons do we get from this vision on the mighty acts of the Holy Spirit in all the spiritual revivals and renewals in the Church today?
6. What should be the attitude of the Church towards regular Holy Spirit revivals and renewals in this end-time period in which we are? Why do we need regular

Holy Ghost revivals in the Church today more than any other time in the history of the church?

7. What are some of the specific Bible passages which talk about the Holy Spirit as our third great source of spiritual revivals and spiritual renewals?

8. What great support does the Holy Spirit offer us when we seek His spiritual revivals and renewals all the time?

9. What great work does the Holy Spirit do for us in connection with the sealing of our salvation?

SOME PRACTICAL WAYS IN WHICH THE HOLY SPIRIT CAN WORK TO BRING US CONTINUOUS SPIRITUAL REVIVALS AND SPIRITUAL RENEWALS

In God's plan, the Holy Spirit has always been the mighty power and great moving force behind all revivals. This means that even though all spiritual revivals and renewals in essence come from God, He actualizes these moves in the personal lives of believers and in the church through the ministry and practical operation of the Holy Spirit. For this reason certain important spiritual concepts and facts must be understood as we talk about the Spiritual revivals and renewals granted by the Holy Spirit to pave the way for us to be able to receive these revivals and renewals freely without any interruptions whenever we desire and pray for them. At least we want to discuss three of these important concepts here as follows:

1. **The spiritual renewals granted by the Holy Spirit are always accompanied by the manifestation of great Holy Ghost power**

   Holy ghost revivals are always a source of the tremendous power of the Holy Spirit. In times of Holy Ghost revival, God makes this new energy available. Our former fruitless efforts now give way to God's striking, breaking and quickening power of the Holy Spirit. This immediately gives birth to a spiritual awakening which impacts lives positively for Christ. In addition to this great display of external power, the new life in Christ is born to become manifest to all. This ultimately leads to a new love for Christ, a new commitment to Christ and a new dedication to the Great Commission.

2. **The spiritual renewals granted by the Holy Spirit always make the Spirit-filled life possible**

   It is often asserted by many theologians and many sincere Christians who have walked with Christ successfully up to the end of their lives that the true Christian life is an impossible life on earth without the full power and enablement of the Holy Spirit. Satan and his demons are always actively working in the world to be able to tempt and bring believers back into their former life of bondage in sin. So if we can continue in the Christian race in holiness and purity and finish it successfully, we also need the omnipotent power of the Holy Spirit to fill us from time to time to help us to get strength, power and victory over all the seductions of the devil and his demons. So truly, the true Christian life can never be possible on earth without the full backing of the mighty power of the Holy Spirit.

3. **The spiritual renewal granted by the Holy Spirit must be conceived as a continuous spiritual process in our walk with God**

    The true Christian life is a walk and a process which begins on the day of your conversion and ends on the day you close your eyes in death. The total number of days and years in this long walk is solely in the hands of the Creator. But as we continue to walk with Him daily towards eternity, we should forever remember the statement of Christ in the gospel of John which says: "…without me, you can do nothing" (John 15:5). This will help us to remember to rely fully on the Holy Spirit and seek His repeated infillings as the apostles always did after Pentecost any time we come up against any spiritual obstacles and impediments to be able to continue and finish this journey towards eternity.

Bible Study and Personal Review Questions
1. What are some of the great events which often accompany all Holy Ghost revivals? What

encouragements should we gather from this to seek regular Holy Ghost revivals?

2. What is the Spirit-filled life? How can we attain and maintain this Spirit-filled life as Christians? What special spiritual benefit can the Spirit-filled life bring to us to be able to live the victorious Christian life?

3. Why is it absolutely important to us today as Christians to be constant in seeking the spiritual revivals, renewals and in-filling of the Holy Spirit? How can this help us to defeat Satan all the time to finish both the Christian race and the Christian journey?

CHAPTER FOUR
THE WORD OF GOD AND GOD'S REVIVALS

INTRODUCTION

As believers and the genuine children of God, the Word of God should always be our guide in whatever we do both as personal individuals and together with other believers as the body of Christ. Revival is such an important subject in the Church of Christ that in exploring it in this section which aims at guiding all the genuine seekers of this revival to be able to discover the exact things to do to receive God's personal and group revivals regularly, we cannot ignore and set aside the word of God. It is only the word of God which can help us to answer all the important questions on revival like "What is revival?", "How do revivals come?" and "How can the church work to sustain God's revivals all the time?"

So we want to discuss some specific Bible passages in this chapter which can give us all the essential facts about the pattern, process and sustenance of God's true revivals from the word of God. This will help us to know that the Bible is not only the foundation of all genuine revivals but also the pillars of any beneficial and lasting spiritual renewals and spiritual restorations in the Church of Christ. We are aiming at handling the discussion in this chapter in three major ways. First, we will talk about the authority of God's word which makes it sensible and needful to rely upon it in our quest for revival. Secondly, we will discuss the pattern for all God-given revivals as revealed in the Scriptures. Thirdly, we will finish off with a discussion of some of the powerful Bible promises on God's revivals and spiritual renewals. Let us start with the question of biblical authority as follows:

THE WORD OF GOD MUST BE ACCEPTED AND REGARDED AS THE ONLY AUTHORITATIVE SOURCE IN ALL MATTERS OF FAITH, PRACTICAL CONDUCT AND CHURCH ACTIVITIES

The desire to seek God's revival either personally or at the general church level always stems from our realization of the truth that we have either veered or are in the process of veering from God's word and its holy standards. This is what ignites the holy desire in us to seek God's revival and renewal and the accompanying restoration. Because of the acceptance of the word of God as the final source of authority in all matters of faith in the Church as well as our spiritual standard and practical guide in all areas of practical Christian living, it is appropriate to stand upon it all the time to check our true spiritual state so that it can act as a mirror to help us to discover our true spiritual condition so as to be able to correct whatever has gone wrong in our lives before Satan takes advantage of us.

This is one of the main reasons why the word of God is always described as the foundation of all true revivals from God. Many people are staying in the Church of Christ today as "unbelieving believers" because by their refusal to submit fully to and bring themselves under the authority of the word of God, they have no guide or sure spiritual standard. Consequently, let us at this juncture discuss fully the question of the authority of the Bible and the bearing this has on the search for spiritual revivals and spiritual renewals in the Church of Christ today.

Bible Study and Personal Review Questions
1. Generally, what is the value of the word of God in our search for God's revival?
2. Why do some theologians describe the word of God as both the foundation and the pillars of God's revival?
3. Why can it be very dangerous to ignore the Word of God in our search for God's true revival? What are some of the essential facts the Bible can help us to discover about God's revivals?

THE MEANING OF BIBLICAL AUTHORITY

To have authority in the human sense is to have the power or right to give orders, make decisions and enforce obedience. So when we talk about the authority of the Bible today, what exactly are we referring to? This means that in the divine plan of God, the Bible has been given this same level of authority in the affairs of all men in general and in all matters in the Church of Christ in particular. The only difference is that the Bible is not a human being but a divinely written document. *The authority of Scripture can therefore be expanded as every word of the Bible possessing the full authority of God and having the right to rule all the minds, hearts and bodies of all the inhabitants of the earth.*

The Bible has this level of universal authority because of the fact that it originated directly from God Himself as the divine creator of mankind to be the guide and the rule of conduct in the lives of all the people He created and brought into the world to inhabit it. *The Bible does not derive its universal authority from any man. Rather, this authority is sourced directly in God Himself as the creator and sustainer of the whole universe which includes human beings.* It is for this reason that Scripture says in 2 Timothy 3:16 that all Scripture is God-breathed which means Scripture is God speaking directly to mankind through some specially selected and prepared persons by His Spirit. So whether mankind accepts this high level of spiritual authority placed on the Bible or not, this does not change anything. Because a thing is true and will forever remain the truth whether or not someone believes it!

Bible Study and Personal Review Questions
1. Is it appropriate to claim "If there is no word of God, there is no revival?" If yes, why? And if no how?
2. What level of universal authority does the holy Bible have?
3. Who is the source of this great universal authority of the Bible? How can this great authority be validated logically today?
4. How can this great authority of the Bible be proved and established theologically?
5. Does it matter whether the world accepts and acknowledges this high level of authority placed on the Bible by God? What is your personal opinion?
6. In what ways can we say that biblical inspiration is one of the greatest proofs of the authority of the Bible?

BIBLICAL INSPIRATION IS A PROOF OF BIBLICAL AUTHORITY

As already explained above, biblical authority does not stand alone. It is proved, strengthened and stratified by the fact that the Bible is a fully inspired divine document. For us to understand what we exactly mean when we talk about the inspiration of the Bible, let us read this simple definition and explanation of inspiration provided by **Jason Jackson.**

What Is Bible "Inspiration"?
What do Bible scholars mean when they speak of the "inspiration" of the Scriptures?
By Jason Jackson

The Bible makes a claim that most books do not. It claims to be from God. Unlike the few that make the claim, the Bible's claim is true. This is the concept called "inspiration." There are several things involved in considering the "inspiration of the Bible."

> *First, "inspiration" of the Bible means that it had a divine origin. The term "inspiration" is found in the New Testament one time (2 Tim. 3:16).*

> *"Every scripture inspired of God is also profitable for teaching, for reproof, for correction, for instruction which is in righteousness." ESV*

The Greek word theopneustos is actually a compound term. Its two parts (theos and pneustos) literally mean "God-breathed." For this reason, English translations render the word by the phrase "inspired of God," rather than just "inspired."

Paul said that scripture is inspired by God. The word "scripture" comes from the Greek term graphe, which means "writings." Paul was considering a specific body of writings. The word "scripture" is used in the Bible in a technical sense to distinguish writings whose origin is God, from those that originate with men. Practically speaking, the terms, "inspired of God" and "scriptures," are interchangeable.

The apostle said that "every" or "all" scripture is from God. When Paul said that "every scripture" is inspired of God, he affirmed that the Law, the Prophets, and the Psalms — the Lord's three-fold designation of the Old Testament (Lk. 24:44) — were all from God. Both Old and New Testaments are called "scripture" (see 1 Tim. 5:18; 2 Pet. 3:15-16; cf. 1 Cor. 2:10-13).

Second, "inspiration of the Bible" means that God used prophetic agency. The writer of Hebrews referred to the human element in scripture when he said, "God, having of old time spoken unto the fathers in the prophets" (Heb. 1:1; emphasis added). The prophets were speaking; they were writing with pen and parchments. But, the words actually were God's.

The apostle Peter noted that "the word of prophecy" was of God's design. In communicating his will, however, "men spake from God, being moved by the Holy Spirit" (2 Pet. 1:21).

The "inspiration" of the human writers did not mean that they were mere transcribers. God employed their human personalities and experiences in the process. Inspired men were not omniscient or personally infallible. But what they wrote was from the mind of God — and it was recorded without error.

They also used firsthand knowledge, the aid of eyewitnesses, and written sources in the composition of Scripture (cf. Lk. 1:1-4). All of these methods, however, were under the guidance of the Holy Spirit, with the guarantee of accuracy (cf. Jn. 16:13).

Third, "inspiration of the Bible" means that this book is authoritative. The Bible is the final word in religious matters. As Paul discussed some doctrinal issues in Romans, he said, "What saith the scriptures?" (Rom. 4:3). The Lord charged the Sadducees, "Ye do err, not knowing the scriptures" (Mt. 22:29). What God has revealed is important when considering any religious matter.

The Bible is the will of God. It is his authoritative word. For that reason, Jesus Christ said, "and the scriptures cannot be broken" (Jn. 10:35). We cannot dismiss God's written word. It is as authoritative as if God spoke directly from heaven (cf. Mt. 22:31; 2 Pet. 1:18-20).

Bible Study and Personal Review Questions
1. What is the first truth we can learn about the inspiration of the Bible and its relation to biblical authority?
2. What level of inspiration did God give to the Bible? Was it full or partial?
3. What is the importance of God's use of holy prophets in the preparation of the Bible to its high level of inspiration and authority?

PROOFS OF THE INSPIRATION AND AUTHORITY OF THE HOLY BIBLE

The Bible does not just claim to be inspired. Upon examination, the Bible provides clear and abundant evidence that it is truly inspired and possesses all the authority conferred upon it by God. The Bible has abundant internal evidence that it is fully inspired and fully authoritative. It also possesses great external evidence that it is fully inspired and fully authoritative. Recent archaeological discoveries which contain documents and stories parallel to the message of the Bible offer us evidence of the inspiration of the authority of the Bible. Another external evidence of the inspiration and authority of the Bible can be found in its numerous fulfilled prophecies including prophecies about the coming messiah; prophecies about great civilizations like Assyria, Babylon, Nineveh, ancient Israel, Persia and so on.

In addition to all these, the Bible further offers us great internal evidence of its inspiration and authority as we are soon going to verify in this section. But because time and space will not permit us to explain and expand every detail of what we are saying, we want to present some of the essential facts on this with the appropriate Scriptural undergirding as follows:

INTERNAL EVIDENCE
1. Scripture's Self-Attestation
   (Psalm 19:1; 2 Timothy 3:16; 2 Peter 1:21)
2. Fulfilled Prophecy
   (Isaiah 44:1, 4, 25)
3. Scripture's Unity
   (2 Peter 1:20-21)
4. Jesus Christ and the Holy Spirit's Recorded Testimonies
   (John 17:17; 16:13; Matthew 5:18; Luke 16:17) (John 5:39; Luke 24:27; 2 Peter 1:20-21)
5. Endurance and Survival of the Scriptures
   The endurance and survival of the Bible against all vicious attacks is one of the proofs of its inspiration and

authority. Up to today, the Bible remains the best-selling book of all time. History, archaeology, and science have confirmed it as true instead of refuting it.

CONCLUDING NOTE

What is the relevance of the authority of the Bible, the inspiration of the Bible and the proofs of authority and inspiration provided at the beginning of this chapter to the question of spiritual revivals, spiritual renewals and spiritual restorations? They are extremely relevant to the question of spiritual revivals because apart from providing the genesis of these renewals, they further provide the foundation and the pillars on which all the true revivals granted by the God-head can comfortably rest to provide the continuous spiritual renewals needed by the Church. This is true because understanding and accepting the divine authority and inspiration of the Scriptures will make it easy for us to submit to this authority and thereby allow it to serve as the spiritual mirror which can show us our true spiritual state all the time.

It is only after knowing this true spiritual state regularly and from time to time that we can recognize our urgent need of God's regular spiritual revivals, spiritual renewals and spiritual restorations. This is why it must be understood that without this knowledge of the spiritual and practical standard of God from the Bible, there can never be any genuine desire and sincere quest and striving for God's valuable and indispensable spiritual revivals, spiritual renewals and spiritual restorations. So the word of God is extremely important in our understanding, seeking, obtaining and maintaining God's spiritual revivals, renewals and restorations.

Bible Study and Personal Review Questions
1. What external proofs are offered in the secular world and in history that the Bible is truly inspired and fully authoritative?
2. What proofs of fulfilled prophecies about Israel, Judah, Samaria, Babylon, Assyria, Persia, and other important ancient peoples can we use today to establish the inspiration and authority of the Bible?
3. What sources of internal evidence do we have to confirm the inspiration and authority of the Bible?

IT IS THE WORD OF GOD ALONE WHICH PROVIDES THE GENUINE PATTERN FOR ALL THE TRUE REVIVALS FROM THE LIVING GOD
The Holy Bible is the divine watershed of everything we need to know and do in Christianity. That is why the Church of Christ must make it dogmatic that if it is not in the Bible then it cannot be in the Church; and if it is not in the Bible then it cannot be in the life of any genuine child

of God! Revivals have always been in the Bible from the Old Testament days up to our present day. Any time the people of God backslide and go wayward, revivals have always been God's principal means of bringing them back to Himself. So revivals can always be said to be both ancient and modern! If this is the case then there is nothing about revivals which we cannot get from the Bible especially the foundation and pattern of revivals which are always essential in all God-given revivals. Let us try to find out what the word of God has to say about these two major components of all God-given revivals in the church of Christ as follows:

Bible Study and Personal Review Questions
1. Is it appropriate to describe the Bible as the "watershed" of true Christianity?
2. What practical deductions can we make from this in the matter of Christian doctrine and practice today?
3. What further deductions can we make from this on the subject of spiritual revivals and renewals?

THE WORD OF GOD AS THE FOUNDATION OF ALL SPIRITUAL REVIVALS

The foundation of a great spiritual concept like revival is the basis or principle upon which it stands to be accessible or effectual. This in other words can be said to be the basic tenets which when understood and properly applied can always lead to our receiving and practically experiencing the mighty revivals of the Holy Spirit. The inference we can make from this is that all God-given revivals can either be delayed or totally denied where this foundation is non-existent. This is the act which gives practical justification to our discussion of the importance of the word of God in our search for spiritual revivals in this chapter. Let us discuss the word of God as the foundation of God's revivals with the following details:

I. We should always plead for God's spiritual revivals and spiritual renewals on the basis of God's word

Psalm 119:25
My soul clings to the dust; revive me according to Your word. NKJV

Psalm 119:107
I am afflicted very much; revive me, O Lord, according to Your word. NKJV

Psalm 119:153-154
Consider my affliction and deliver me, for I do not forget Your law. Plead my cause and redeem me; revive me according to Your word. NKJV

II. After doing this, we should be positive to expect all the blessings of God's spiritual revivals and renewals to come to us
Psalm 119:50

This is my comfort in my affliction, for Your word has given me life. NKJV

Psalm 119: 74, 116

Those who fear You will be glad when they see me, because I have hoped in Your word. Uphold me according to Your word, that I may live; and do not let me be ashamed of my hope. NKJV

Psalm 119:130

The entrance of Your words gives light; it gives understanding to the simple. NKJV

Psalm 119:169-170

Let my cry come before You, O Lord; give me understanding according to Your word. Let my supplication come before You; deliver me according to Your word. NKJV

Psalm 119:81

My soul faints for Your salvation, but I hope in Your word. NKJV

Bible Study and Personal Review Questions

1. What are we specifically referring to when we say that the Word of God is the foundation of all revivals?

2. How can our misunderstanding the word of God as the foundation of God's revivals either lead to the delay or total denial of God's revivals in our lives?
3. What are the two major steps we should always take to make the word of God the true foundation of the spiritual revival we desire?

THE WORD OF GOD AS THE PATTERN OF ALL SPIRITUAL REVIVALS

The pattern of anything is the acceptable design or model (copy, duplicate, sample) used in making things. In other words, the pattern of anything will always give you a replica or picture of what that thing should be and exactly how it should look like when it is finally fashioned. So the biblical pattern of all genuine God-given revivals must be known and understood before we start crying to God for any such revivals so that Satan the great deceiver can never lead us astray to move away from God's spiritual and practical standards. This will also help us not to pray amiss in our search for God's true spiritual revivals and spiritual renewals. To help us understand the pattern the word of God has provided for all Holy Ghost inspired revivals in the Church of Christ, let us examine the following passage from Psalm 119:26-32.

Psalm 119:26-32

I gave an account of my ways and you answered me; teach me your decrees. Cause me to understand the way of your precepts, that I may meditate on your wonderful deeds. My soul is weary with sorrow; strengthen me according to your word. Keep me from deceitful ways; be gracious to me and teach me your law. I have chosen the way of faithfulness; I have set my heart on your laws. I hold fast to your statutes, Lord; do not let me be put to shame. I run in the path of your commands, for you have broadened my understanding. NIV

Every good and beneficial thing in life has got its pattern, process and procedure for acquisition. As already explained in the introductory notes, knowing the processes and the procedures for attaining God's spiritual revivals and spiritual renewals are of vital importance because of their capacity to lead us to access God's spiritual revivals and renewals regularly. One of these effective biblical patterns for God's spiritual revivals and renewals can be outlined, carefully studied and always followed in the passage quoted above with the following details:

1. Begin your search for God's revival with genuine penitence for your shortcomings followed by open confession.

"I gave an account of my ways and you answered me; teach me your decrees." NIV (Psalm 119:26)

2. Our revival prayer must also include prayer for deep spiritual understanding of all the ways of God.

   "Help me understand the meaning of your commandments, and I will meditate on your wonderful deeds." NLT (Psalm 119:27)

3. Our revival prayer must also focus on the renewal of our spiritual strength.

   "My soul is weary with sorrow; strengthen me according to your word." NIV (Psalm 119:28)

4. Our revival prayer must include prayer for victory over our habitual sins.

   "Keep me from lying to myself; give me the privilege of knowing your instructions." NLT (Psalm 119:29)

5. Our revival prayer must include the prayer for total spiritual rededication and full commitment.

   "I have chosen to be faithful; I have determined to live by your regulations." NLT (Psalm 119:30)

6. We should specifically pray for God's favour and mercy. Our prayer for revival must include our rededication to the standards and precepts of God's word.

   "I hold fast to your statutes, Lord; do not let me be put to shame." NIV (Psalm 119:31)

7. The prayer for revival must include the renewal of our dedication to a life of holiness and obedience to God's righteous standards.

   "I will pursue your commands, for you expand my understanding." NLT (Psalm 119:32)

Bible Study and Personal Review Questions

1. What does it exactly mean to say that the Word of God is the pattern of all true spiritual revivals?
2. As the pattern of God's revivals, what help does the Word of God offer us to know what to ask for when praying for God's spiritual revivals and renewals?
3. Without maintaining the Word of God as the pattern of God's revivals, can we always remain on the right path to God's revivals and spiritual renewals? What can happen to us and what can be some of its fatal spiritual consequences?

THE WORD OF GOD HAS GIVEN US ALL THE IMPORTANT PROMISES WE NEED ON GOD'S SPIRITUAL REVIVAL

The Bible is not only a book of theology. It is also a book of hope and firm promises and assurances on our receiving God's continuous revivals whenever the need arises for this. This is one of the many practical reasons which have made the Bible relevant to all the different peoples of the world wherever they are throughout all the generations and dispensations of the world. What it says on revivals in the Holy Bible is one of the encouraging truths which have given us the full hope and assurance of receiving God's sure revivals through continuous prevailing prayer after initially repenting and turning away from sin. We want to conclude this chapter by looking at some of these important promises on God's revivals to encourage us in our search for God's genuine spiritual renewal and restoration. Some of these great promises on revival can be grouped from the Bible as follows:

THE WORD OF GOD PROVIDES US WITH THE ASSURANCE OF GOD'S REVIVAL

One great benefit the word of God renders to spiritual revivals which make it indispensable in the search for true spiritual revival and renewal is the knowledge and assurance it offers us on the possibility of receiving the regular spiritual renewals of Christ any time we sense any temptations to spiritual lukewarmness. This is a great benefit from God's word because it is this which gives us the encouragement and hope to do whatever is needful to crave after God's genuine spiritual revivals and renewals. Some of these assurances and encouragements have been quoted and put together for our perusal and practical application in the search for God's genuine spiritual revivals and renewals as follows:

Psalm 85:4 (Assurance 1)
"Restore us again, O God of our salvation, and put away your indignation toward us!" NIV

Psalm 119:25 (Assurance 2)
I am laid low in the dust; preserve my life according to your word. NIV

Lamentations 5:21 (Assurance 3)
Restore us to yourself, Lord, that we may return; renew our days as of old. NIV

Habakkuk 3:2 (Assurance 4)
Lord, I have heard of your fame; I stand in awe of your deeds, Lord. Repeat them in our day, in our time make them known; in wrath remember mercy. NIV

Hosea 5:15 (Assurance 5)
Then I will return to my lair until they have borne their guilt and seek my face — in their misery they will earnestly seek me." NIV

Psalm 80:14-15 (Assurance 6)

Return to us, God Almighty! Look down from heaven and see! Watch over this vine, the root your right hand has planted, the son you have raised up for yourself. NIV

<u>Psalm 85:4-7</u> (Assurance 7)
Restore us again, God our Savior, and put away your displeasure toward us. Will you be angry with us forever? Will you prolong your anger through all generations? Will you not revive us again, that your people may rejoice in you? Show us your unfailing love, Lord, and grant us your salvation. NIV

<u>Jeremiah 31:18</u> (Assurance 8)
"I have surely heard Ephraim's moaning: 'You disciplined me like an unruly calf, and I have been disciplined. Restore me, and I will return, because you are the Lord my God. NIV

<u>Isaiah 55:1-3</u> (Assurance 9)
"Come, all you who are thirsty, come to the waters; and you who have no money, come, buy and eat! Come, buy wine and milk without money and without cost Why spend money on what is not bread, and your labor on what does not satisfy? Listen, listen to me, and eat what is good, and you will delight in the richest of fare. Give ear and come to me; listen, that you may live. I will make an everlasting covenant with you, my faithful love promised to David. NIV

<u>Jeremiah 3:22</u> (Assurance 10)

"Return, faithless people; I will cure you of backsliding." "Yes, we will come to you, for you are the Lord our God. NIV

Lamentations 3:40 (Assurance 11)
Let us examine our ways and test them, and let us return to the Lord. NIV

Hosea 12:6 (Assurance 12)
But you must return to your God; maintain love and justice, and wait for your God always. NIV

Hosea 14:1-2 (Assurance 13)
Return, Israel, to the Lord your God. Your sins have been your downfall! Take words with you and return to the Lord. Say to him: "Forgive all our sins and receive us graciously, that we may offer the fruit of our lips. NIV

Zechariah 1:3 (Assurance 14)
Therefore tell the people: This is what the Lord Almighty says: 'Return to me,' declares the Lord Almighty, 'and I will return to you,' says the Lord Almighty. NIV

Malachi 3:7 (Assurance 15)
Ever since the time of your ancestors you have turned away from my decrees and have not kept them. Return to me, and I will return to you," says the Lord Almighty. "But you ask, 'How are we to return?' NIV

What should we say after going through this list of Bible references encouraging us to seek God's spiritual revivals? The message is simple: REVIVAL IS POSSIBLE FOR ALL THOSE WHO SINCERELY DESIRE IT AND ARE PREPARED TO WORK TOWARDS IT! Though revival is important for all in the Church, God has not made it compulsory for everybody. It is there. But it is given only to all those who see that they need it after going through encouraging references such as are listed above and are prepared to work towards it.

Bible Study and Personal Review Questions
1. It is accurate to say that generally, the Bible is our greatest source of assurance as far as God's revivals and renewals are concerned?
2. How can we stand upon this to describe the Bible as a book of hope and assurance?
3. What are some of the specific assurances of God's revival and renewal we have in the numerous references listed here?
4. What positive truths are contained in each of these numerous references to encourage us that it is possible to obtain God's spiritual revivals and renewals today?
5. After putting your name into places where nouns and pronouns occur in these assurances, what personal effect do you get that it is possible for you also to seek

and receive God's personal revival immediately? What are you going to do about this and when?

THE WORD OF GOD CONTAINS THE GENERAL CONDITIONS FOR GOD'S REVIVAL

There are always some conditions and requirements attached to all the good things in life whether they are mainly spiritual or purely material. Clouds have to form before we can receive any rains. The sun has to shine before we can receive light. Similarly, the general conditions and requirements attached to God's outpouring of His spiritual revivals must be met before they can be poured down upon us. In addition to the many promises and assurances given to us on the possibility of receiving God's spiritual revivals and spiritual renewals, here are some of the important Bible references which spell out some of the important general conditions attached to these revivals. Some of them can be quoted and put together as follows:

> 2 Chronicles 7:14 (Condition 1)
> *If My people who are called by My name will humble themselves, and pray and seek My face, and turn from their wicked ways, then I will hear from heaven, and will forgive their sin and heal their land.*
> NIV

> Isaiah 57:15 (Condition 2)

For this is what the high and exalted One says — he who lives forever, whose name is holy: "I live in a high and holy place, but also with the one who is contrite and lowly in spirit, to revive the spirit of the lowly and to revive the heart of the contrite. NIV

Matthew 6:33 (Condition 3)
But seek first his kingdom and his righteousness, and all these things will be given to you as well. NIV

Acts 3:19-20 (Condition 4)
Repent, then, and turn to God, so that your sins may be wiped out, that times of refreshing may come from the Lord, and that he may send the Messiah, who has been appointed for you — even Jesus. NIV

James 4:8 (Condition 5)
Come near to God and he will come near to you. Wash your hands, you sinners, and purify your hearts, you double-minded. NIV

Isaiah 66:2 (Condition 6)
Has not my hand made all these things, and so they came into being?" declares the Lord. "These are the ones I look on with favor: those who are humble and contrite in spirit, and who tremble at my word. NIV

Revelation 2:5 (Condition 7)

Consider how far you have fallen! Repent and do the things you did at first. If you do not repent, I will come to you and remove your lampstand from its place. NIV

<u>Joel 2:12-13</u> (Condition 8)
"Even now," declares the Lord, "return to me with all your heart, with fasting and weeping and mourning." Rend your heart and not your garments. Return to the Lord your God, for he is gracious and compassionate, slow to anger and abounding in love, and he relents from sending calamity. NIV

<u>Deuteronomy 4:29</u> (Condition 9)
But if from there you seek the Lord your God, you will find him if you seek him with all your heart and with all your soul. NIV

One major reason why so many people fail to receive God's regular spiritual revivals and renewals is not because they do not need them but mainly because THEY ALWAYS FAIL TO DO WHAT CAN BRING THESE REVIVALS AND RENEWALS TO THEM. The nine Bible verses listed here are meant to help all such people to know precisely what they have to do towards God for Him to pour His spiritual revivals and renewals upon them. Do you see that you also need God's spiritual revivals immediately? Then go further by applying the conditions listed above and all shall be well.

Bible Study and Personal Review Questions

1. What do we specifically call a condition whether spiritual or physical? What proofs do we have that the fulfilment of conditions is a normal part of life?
2. Have you ever personally fulfilled some conditions in life before obtaining some precious things? What were the conditions and what did you obtain after fulfilling them?
3. What do you see as the first major condition of revival after reading through all the references here?
4. What additional conditions on receiving God's spiritual revivals and renewals do you gather from these numerous references?
5. In both the spiritual realm and in practical life, what makes it totally impossible on the part of our holy God to grant us His revivals without our first fulfilling these conditions?
6. If you truly desire God's revival at the personal level, what must you start doing about these conditions immediately?

THE WORD OF GOD CONTAINS ALL OUR BLESSINGS AND REWARDS AFTER RECEIVING GOD'S REVIVALS

The Lord God assures us in Matthew 7:7 in the great matter of prayer just as it is in all the other major spiritual activities of the Christian life, that whenever we do what is needful and search for Him we can surely find Him and receive the genuine and beneficial desires of our hearts. "Ask and it will be given to you; seek and you will find; knock and the door will be opened to you." (Matthew 7:7). This means that if you sincerely desire God's spiritual revival and renewal and you go further to do the needful to open the door for this to come, then surely you can receive this desire of your heart with its accompanying multiple blessings. The following references reveal some of the important blessings and privileges which we can gain and inherit as follows:

Psalm 80:3 (Blessing 1)
Restore us, O God; make your face shine on us, that we may be saved. NIV

Psalm 80:18 (Blessing 2)
Then we will not turn away from you; revive us, and we will call on your name. NIV

Psalm 149:4 (blessings 3)
For the Lord takes delight in his people; he crowns the humble with victory. NIV

Jeremiah 24:7 (Blessings 4)

I will give them a heart to know me, that I am the Lord. They will be my people, and I will be their God, for they will return to me with all their heart. NIV

<u>Hebrews 8:10</u> (Blessing 5)
This is the covenant I will establish with the people of Israel after that time, declares the Lord. I will put my laws in their minds and write them on their hearts. I will be their God, and they will be my people. NIV

<u>Ezekiel 11:19, 20</u> (Blessing 6)
I will give them an undivided heart and put a new spirit in them; I will remove from them their heart of stone and give them a heart of flesh. Then they will follow my decrees and be careful to keep my laws. They will be my people, and I will be their God. NIV

<u>Exodus 36:4-7</u> (Blessing 7)
So all the skilled workers who were doing all the work on the sanctuary left what they were doing and said to Moses, "The people are bringing more than enough for doing the work the Lord commanded to be done." Then Moses gave an order and they sent this word throughout the camp: "No man or woman is to make anything else as an offering for the sanctuary." And so the people were restrained from

bringing more, because what they already had was more than enough to do all the work. NIV

<u>1 Chronicles 29:6-9</u> (Blessing 8)
Then the leaders of families, the officers of the tribes of Israel, the commanders of thousands and commanders of hundreds, and the officials in charge of the king's work gave willingly. They gave toward the work on the temple of God five thousand talents and ten thousand darics of gold, ten thousand talents of silver, eighteen thousand talents of bronze and a hundred thousand talents of iron. Anyone who had precious stones gave them to the treasury of the temple of the Lord in the custody of Jehiel the Gershonite. The people rejoiced at the willing response of their leaders, for they had given freely and wholeheartedly to the Lord. David the king also rejoiced greatly. NIV

<u>Acts 11:28-30</u> (Blessing 9)
One of them, named Agabus, stood up and through the Spirit predicted that a severe famine would spread over the entire Roman world. (This happened during the reign of Claudius.) The disciples, as each one was able, decided to provide help for the brothers and sisters living in Judea. This they did, sending their gift to the elders by Barnabas and Saul. NIV

Deuteronomy 30:2-3 (Blessing 10)
And when you and your children return to the Lord your God and obey him with all your heart and with all your soul according to everything I command you today, then the Lord your God will restore your fortunes and have compassion on you and gather you again from all the nations where he scattered you. NIV

This is the most joyful and enjoyable portions on all discussions on God's spiritual revivals and renewals because they contain most of the amazing blessings and rewards which naturally follow all true spiritual revivals and spiritual awakenings. We all want good and rosy things both in the physical and practical realms but such rosy things always come to us only after periods of great effort, hard work and even sometimes sacrifice. The good news here is that when we make every effort to receive and maintain God's genuine revivals and further do everything possible to protect these revivals, the numerous blessings from God will always follow us. The blessings always come in multiples and affect all the major areas of life and existence on earth. Truly, our God is good!

Bible Study and Personal Review Questions
1. What are some of the things which can be described as "blessings" spiritually, physically and materially?

2. Though we all need these blessings regularly, why are they sometimes withheld from us by God?

3. After carefully reading these references, how many types and levels of blessings can you identify?

4. How many of these blessings do you see in your life as a Christian today?

5. How many of these blessings are absent in your life? Why are you also not receiving them and enjoying them fully as a Christian? What has gone wrong? And what are the possible remedies and corrections for this?

6. Will you conclude after going through these references that it is important for us as Christians to seek God's revivals constantly with our whole hearts?